MORE STAR STEEDS AND OTHER DREAMS
THE COLLECTED POEMS
NEW, EXPANDED EDITION

Dr Karl P.N. Shuker

Typeset by Jonathan Downes,
©Cover and Layout by SPiderKaT for CFZ Communications
Using Microsoft Word 2000, Microsoft , Publisher 2000, Adobe Photoshop CS.

First published in Great Britain by Fortean Words

CFZ Press
Myrtle Cottage
Woolsery
Bideford
North Devon
EX39 5QR

© CFZ MMXV

ISBN: 978-1-909488-38-0

DEDICATION

For my little blond-haired blue-eyed brother, André (27 October 1955 – 3 December 1955), whose passing four years before I was born meant that I could never share any of his short stay on Earth, or offer him a gift of anything, until now.

I have been a seeker of strange animals for many years as an adult, and also a writer of possibly even stranger verses, especially as a lean, mullet-haired, dream-headed youth – enthused with high hopes and even greater expectations for the future.

Whatever happened to that youth, I wonder, and whatever would André have thought of him? I hope with all my heart that he would have approved, and that he would have found pleasure in these poems.

We never met in this world, little bro, but, God willing, we shall meet in the next and I shall also be reunited there at last with our dear little Mom and the rest of our family, which will be truly wonderful.

PIC: The author with his West Highland white terrier puppy, Sam, back in 1981.
(© Dr Karl Shuker)

List of Contents

A Phantasia of Ghosts and Illusions
Reflections in the Mirror
The Shadow
Sleep
Snow Dreaming
Starlight Fantasia
The Voice of the Winds
The Windmill
Worlds of Faerie

Part 3 – A Sense of Mystery
Ballet of the Willows
Behold the Thunder Horse
The Bomb
Fairy Lullaby
Flying Horse Fantasia
The Flying Saucer
The Haunted Cottage
The Loch Ness Monster
Oberon's Garden
Perchance a Mermaid?
The Pool of Dreams
The Star Horse
Stonehenge
Transforming the Dragon
A Tribute to Quetzalcoatl
The Unicorn / Dragons / Tattoos / Mirabilis / The Panther

Part 4 – Looking Forward, Looking Back
Borne Into Tomorrow
A Call From My Past
The Clown
Dismissing Childhood
A Ghost From The Past
Patch – A Four-Legged Friend
Reflections of Summers Past
Remembering the Woodlands
Robin
The Rose Garden
The Scientists
The Silence of Solitude
A Silver Jubilee Tribute
Thoughts of a Dreamer
Yesterday's Street

Part 5 – The Glory of God
The Angel
As Bright as the Waterfall
The Christmas Donkey
Fields of Remembrance
Heaven's Bell
Here Comes Another Rainy Day
Life – The Infinity of the World
The Mole and the Fieldmouse
The Monastery Garden
The Music of the Spheres
The Robin and the Crossbill
The Swan of Tuonela
The Transformation of Saint Eustacius
What is God?
The Wild Roses
Wonders Untold

Part 6 – Younger Days
The Balloon
The Butterfly
The Church / The Churchyard
Fireworks – Bright Flowers of the Night
The Forget-Me-Not
The Mole
The Monastery
Mother Nature
Nod
Papillon
Polperro
The Weeping Willow Tree
White Star

Part 7 – Time To Say Goodbye
Airport
And Forever Shall I Wait For You
Elvina
Endings
A Last Visit
The Last Morning
The Parting
Reborn
Worlds Apart
Yesterday No Longer – The Seashore By Twilight

INTRODUCTION
TIME FOR A RHYME

Poetry is the journal of the sea animal living on land, wanting to fly in the air. Poetry is a search for syllables to shoot at the barriers of the unknown and the unknowable. Poetry is a phantom script telling how rainbows are made and why they go away.

Carl Sandburg - *Poetry Considered*

I t isn't always easy to remember when or how exactly a lifelong passion began, but as far as my undiminished love of poetry is concerned, I can date its origin precisely – to that magical, life-changing day when, as an 8-year-old child, my mother bought me a certain book. It was a wonderful anthology entitled *The Golden Treasury of Poetry*, containing over 400 poems selected by Louis Untermeyer, accompanied with delightful illustrations by Joan Walsh Anglund – and which I still own today, well-thumbed and a little dog-eared but as treasured now as it has always been. Until then, I had read various poems at school and had enjoyed them, but when confronted with hundreds of diverse, captivating verses on every conceivable subject all contained within the covers of a single book, I was totally spellbound.

Here, for the first time, I was introduced to such literary marvels as William Blake's 'Tyger, Tyger', Percy Bysshe Shelley's 'Ozymandias', John Keats's 'La Belle Dame Sans Merci', William Wordsworth's 'Daffodils', Alfred Noyes's 'The Highwayman', Sara Henderson Hay's 'The Shape God Wears', Christina Rossetti's ''Remember Me', W.B. Yeats's 'The Song of Wandering Aengus', Rudyard Kipling's 'If', Samuel Taylor Coleridge's 'Kubla Khan', the nonsense poems of Edward Lear and Lewis Carroll, the quirky nature poems of Emily Dickinson, the prefabulous animiles of James Reeves, and so much more. Soon I could recite many of them in the same easy way that I knew all of the words to my favourite songs, and I delighted in their rhythms and rhymes, in the evocative images conjured forth by their rich vocabulary, and in the ready escape to other worlds where their mesmerising words instantly transported me whenever I read them.

In short, my imagination was fired by poetry in a way that I had never experienced before, and, inevitably, it was not long before I began experimenting with writing poems myself. Much as I still enjoyed reading the verses of others, I now knew that this was no longer enough – I had to express in written form the rhymes and images that were welling forth in my head. And so, as an early teenager, I began to pen poetry in earnest, and continued doing so in prolific quantity until my early 20s. By then, however, other, more pressing literary demands had begun to require and receive my full attention, including university work and my first forays into freelance non-fiction writing. By the time that my first cryptozoological book and articles were published during the late 1980s, my poetry writing had all but ceased, and my folders of poems were tucked away in a bedroom bookcase, where they remained in quiet obscurity for more than two decades.

Just over a year ago, however, I noticed them there, took them out again, and began to read – and suddenly, the years simply melted away and I found myself remembering words that I had written so long ago that I had thought them forgotten forever. But no, they were still there, both on the page and in my memory, as if I had merely stepped outside for a moment and left the folders open on my desk, awaiting my swift return – a return that in reality had taken well over 20 years.

After painstakingly reading through every poem, I was not surprised to find that, with such an expanse of time separating the present day from the younger, bygone age when I had originally written them, some were very self-indulgent, and certain others less than technically adept (their youthful zeal notwithstanding). However, there were also a surprising number that seemed undiminished by the passing of time – but then, as their author, I suppose I would say that! Consequently, I handed out a number of these to a variety of friends and colleagues (including my agent Mandy Little of Watson, Little Limited in London), and at the risk of never speaking to them again should they be too acerbic in their responses, I asked them to comment unreservedly on whether they considered these poems worthy of publication.

Remarkably, I received an unequivocal affirmation from all concerned. Yes, they felt that these were indeed worthy of publication, and so, to cut a not-very-long story even shorter, when Jon Downes of the CFZ Press kindly expressed an interest in doing just that, the present book was born. Only a single modern-day poem of mine, penned just a few months ago, is included here – 'The Mirror of Mnemosyne', written specifically to explain what was at that time planned to be the book's title, but which has since been changed, to link instead with the delightful illustration used on the front cover. All of the others were originally penned during the mid-1970s to early 1980s (though a few of these have been modified slightly in more recent times). Moreover, as you will see, I have written on numerous subjects, in a variety of different styles, and there is one section devoted entirely to various poems that I have prepared specifically for children. You will also discover that personification of inanimate objects and concepts occurs frequently in my poetry, so look out for plenty of deliberate capitalisations, e.g. Time, Night, Eternity, etc.

One aspect of writing poetry that particularly appeals to me is the creation of word pictures, i.e. converting images and scenes into verbal descriptions. As a result, you will find that many of my poems are very descriptive in form, emphasising colours, movement, subtle changes of light, and other overtly visual facets of the world, and often have little storyline. I appreciate that this may not be to everyone's taste, but as this book contains the most personal, intimate writings of mine ever to have been published, these poems wholly embody my own writing style rather than adhering to one dictated or thrust upon me by any outside influence or convention.

For many people out there, especially those familiar with my cryptozoological writings, they may well assume that writing poetry is a new venture for me, a sequel of sorts to my non-fiction work or even a total departure, a new path taken by me leading away from my traditional publications. In reality, however, as you will now know having read this introduction (and which is the reason why I have written it in this explanatory, autobiographical style), my poetry is not a sequel but a prequel – that is, an early, pre-cryptozoological line of literary endeavour that was ultimately out-competed for my attention by my cryptozoological writings (although in my *Dragons* book I was able to revive to a certain extent my earlier, scientifically-unconstrained, imaginative style of writing when retelling various dragon-related myths and legends).

Had this not happened, who can say what I would have been writing today, what my previous publications (if any) would have been, and even what directions my entire life would have taken? In a sense, it is like speculating what route the evolution of life on earth would have taken if, for example, the mammalian lineage had been out-competed by some other animal group, or if the dinosaurs had not been annihilated by the end of the Cretaceous Period (cryptozoological examples excepted, of course!).

Anyway, such flights of speculative fancy aside, in 2009 I was only too delighted to receive and eagerly grasp the opportunity extended to me by CFZ Press to present at long last the first product of my 'other' line of literary evolution, resurrected from premature extinction and granted a life beyond the confines of some long-forgotten folders in a bedroom bookcase. I hoped that readers would enjoy *Star Steeds and Other Dreams*, and that they would forgive any youthful over-exuberances, naivety, or precocity that they may encounter in it, and I thanked them in advance for what I fervently prayed would be their genuine interest in experiencing this very different book of mine.

Six years later, I am happy to say that all of my hopes and prayers have been met, with my book having proved popular and selling steadily ever since its publication. Moreover, its success has inspired me to renew writing poetry, and even to extend my style repertoire, having since penned a number of semi-rhyming and non-rhyming free-verse poems in addition to ones in my traditional rhyming format. Consequently, CFZ Press and I have now decided to release a new, expanded edition of my book, containing all of the original edition's content plus a diverse selection of my more recent poems, which are presented in two additional thematic sections, of which the final one is devoted to my dear mother, Mary Doreen Shuker. Her passing away in April 2013 was and will always remain the most devastating event of my life, but it also impelled me to preserve for all time my wonderful memories, heartfelt thanks, and above all my absolute love for the best person I shall ever know.

I have entitled this expanded edition *More Star Steeds and Other Dreams*, and as with its original version I wholeheartedly hope that you will enjoy reading it, and also that you may perhaps glimpse the Karl Shuker that exists beyond the rarefied realm of cryptozoology.

> The poet, as everyone knows, must strike his individual note sometime between the ages of fifteen and twenty-five. He may hold it a long time, or a short time, but it is then that he must strike it or never. School and college have been conducted with the almost express purpose of keeping him busy with something else till the danger of his ever creating anything is past.
>
> Robert Frost

PART 1:
WHAT A WONDERFUL WORLD

My poetry has been inspired by a myriad of different themes and subjects, but none more evocative and empowering than the glory and wonder of the natural world, and in particular the rich diversity of its wildlife.

The little cares that fretted me,
I lost them yesterday,
Among the fields above the sea,
Among the winds at play,
Among the lowing of the herds,
The rustling of the trees,
Among the singing of the birds,
The humming of the bees.

The foolish fears of what might pass
I cast them all away
Among the clover-scented grass
Among the new-mown hay,
Among the hushing of the corn
Where drowsy poppies nod,
Where ill thoughts die and good are born –
Out in the fields with God.

Anonymous – 'Out in the Fields with God'

Above all others, we should protect and hold sacred those types, Nature's masterpieces, which are first singled out for destruction on account of their size, or splendour, or rarity, and that false detestable glory which is accorded to their most successful slayers. In ancient times the spirit of life shone brightest in these; and when others that shared the earth with them were taken by death they were left, being more worthy of perpetuation. Like immortal flowers they have drifted down to us on the ocean of time, and their strangeness and beauty bring to our imaginations a dream and a picture of that unknown world, immeasurably far removed, where man was not; and when they perish, something of gladness goes out from nature, and the sunshine loses something of its brightness.

W.H. Hudson – *The Naturalist in La Plata*

The disturbing prospect that, despite our (allegedly) superior brainpower, humanity may now be further from God than are any of His other creations is the basis for this poem – a celebration of the purity and beauty of the wildlife all around us.

The Beautiful People

Blameless and fair are the infants of Nature,
Freed from Temptation and born without Care.
They are unblemished, untainted by Evil;
Mankind they heed not, for Eden is theirs –

Nature unparalleled, Beauty unending,
Radiant Kingdoms from which we are gone.
We were too weak, and Temptation destroyed us;
Fallen, we left, and were forced to pass on,

Lonely and shameful in exile unending,
Banished forever from that which was ours.
They were more wise, and sought only to follow
God and His Mercy, His Truth, and His Power.

Swallows skim brightly like throbbing pulsations
Soaring and gliding in infinite flight,
Rising forever through heavenly strata,
Shooting and streaming like spirits of Light.

Squirrels chase wildly through branches and treetops,
Russet infernos with flushes of flame,
Tails curling brightly like flickering candles,
Darting like fire in arboreal games.

Miniature harvest mice scurry through cornfields,
Tiny brown atoms of scampering joy;
Shyly inquisitive bundles of mischief,
Bustling with life like diminutive toys.

Mottled fawns lie 'neath the woodlands' green mantle,
Secretive denizens, peaceful and shy;
Perfectly camouflaged, dappled by Nature,
Watching her kingdom through dark wary eyes.

Mayflies flit gently like riverside sylvans,
Briefly they mate before sinking to die.
Short is their life, yet infused with rare beauty,
Born in the new when the old flutters by.

Thus they continue while mankind grows feeble,
Lovely they still are, and ever will be.
Fair and unchanging, the beautiful people,
They are His children – the wild, and the free.

Whenever I see a host of dandelion clocks gusting by in the breeze, I think of a whirling ballet of tiny dancers, twirling and spinning in a joyful celebration of nature, and of life itself, however brief it may be.

Dandelion Clocks

Like a fairy ballerina
Dancing softly through the trees,
Gliding silently through Summer
On the laughter of the breeze.

Waltzing gaily 'cross the meadows
As the hours just flutter by,
Twirling swiftly through the woodlands
Like a spotlight from the sky,

Pirouetting round their branches
In a cloud of gauzy dreams,
Rising gently through the shadows
On the sun's auroral beams.

Drifting long with other dancers
From this ballet of the trees,
Like a host of fairy stardust
Scattered far through fields and leas,

Till the heavens' sapphire summer
Is transformed to autumn grey.
Now they're gone, like cloudy snowflakes,
Having danced their lives away.

As Rudyard Kipling's Jungle Books *were among my favourite novels as a child (and still are today), I have little doubt that my floral metaphors for fire in this poem owe something to Kipling's animals referring to it as the Red Flower, a comparison that provides great scope for creative writing.*

Fire

The bright flower of Evil, an orchid of flame,
The hot, scorching wingtip of Death,
Which vanquishes forests, and homesteads, and woods
With gusts of its venomous breath.

A flicker of crimson that blossoms and grows,
With petals that quiver and curl,
Which dazzles the eyes of the onlooking world
As its beauty it swiftly unfurls.

But touch not this shimmering creeper of Death,
A garland of scarlet and flame,
A glittering steed with a bright fiery mane,
And a temper that no-one can tame.

An omen of terror, a lustre of heat,
Whose plumes dart up faster and higher,
A dread, burnished lover whose passion ne'er ends,
For this is the fragrance of fire.

Although much of my poetry is of the rhyming variety, I have ventured from time to time into the less constrained world of prose, as with this composition.

The Fly

A vibrant whirring of wings filled the room, and I gazed up to see a
large, bewildered fly whirling wildly round and round in dizzy,
eccentric circles, periodically crashing into the
deceptively transparent freedom of the windows, only to buzz around
once more in unceasing, dazed convolutions.

"Kill it!" I thought, spearing it with dark, forbidding eyes like chilling
sabres of death, as it spiralled above like a demented spirit drawn ever
downward to damnation, pausing momentarily to wring its suckered
appendages in expressionless despair.

But as my arm rose like a shadowed scythe of fear, the hopelessness of
its plight enveloped me, and I sat back as if I were a lonely silhouette
bowing before the inevitability of Fate, for I was stricken by the
similarity of our twin existences.

Why, are we not from parallel worlds? You – from an outward
macroworld, while I grope ever through an inward microworld. For I
too am continually searching for the knowledge of my own fate,
chasing alone through the endless channels and lonely
corridors of my own mind, seemingly devoid of hope beneath such
curtains of gloom, searching for that which eludes me, passing through
empty chambers of nothingness

This is my unknown, this is my Eternity – an eternity of hopeless
dreams of fulfilment. A door lies open, a mirror lies within, and
from its glass-illuminated interior a colourful circus clown gazes
out. But the clown is weeping, for I myself am peering into the
mirror – a mirror reflecting only my innermost feelings and beliefs.

And as I look, eyes bear down upon me, and faces appear. The
world is watching, and waiting. People are murmuring, and raucous
laughter surrounds me. Where am I to go? Only Fate can tell me.
Yet I am unable to ask.

And so the world continues, the people turn away, finding some
other source of amusement, while I am left to chase ever on through
the phantoms of my own melancholia.

Thus my sympathy, little fly, is yours – we are both lost in alien
worlds. Mine is of my own making, mine to endure. But yours may
be replaced by your natural realm via my
intervention, for yours I see through inward-reflecting
mirrors, though you can never hope to see mine through your
myriad-faceted orbs. Mine is yours inversely, and where they meet,
there one day someone shall find the ultimate Truth.

So leave now, and forget the unforgettable. Why should we both
suffer? Why should one stranger die by the hand of
another?

I slowly arose again, almost as if I were a vast statue
awakened from a deep sleep of petrification, and moved
forward.

I raised my hand like a crescendo of silver trumpets, I opened the
window and let the fly go.

When Martha Washington, a small grey dove-like bird, died in a cage at Cincinnati Zoo on 1 September 1914, her passing marked one of the most shameful episodes in the history of humankind – the extinction of the passenger pigeon, which, incredibly, had been just a century earlier the most abundant species of wild bird in the world, whose vast numbers as witnessed in enormous flocks migrating each year through the North American skies could be counted in the billions, until they were decimated by hunters. This poem is a tribute to that lost bird, and a stark reminder of the inconceivable wickedness responsible for its extermination. The final verse's last word, 'fly', deliberately breaks the tradition set throughout the poem of 'sky' being the last word in each verse, in order to underline a change of direction in the poem, from realism to mysticism.

A Memorial to the Passenger Pigeon

Each year, across the New World sky,
Would flocks of birds in millions fly –
Unending flights eclipsing light
While travelling through the sky.

Known as passenger pigeons, they –
The birds that hid the sun's bright ray
For days and nights while endless flights
Migrated through the sky.

But hunters saw this awesome sight
As food for sport in wild delight,
And shot to kill as ever still
More birds passed through the sky.

Huge raucous clouds of birds in flight,
All unsuspecting of their plight,
Were seen and shot, then left to rot,
As more soared through the sky.

The heavens filled with countless birds,
And through the lands their cries were heard,
As they flew past, upon their last
Migration through the sky.

The pigeons' flocks were soon reduced
When men with savage guns were loosed –
Who aimed and fired, and ne'er grew tired
Of shooting at the sky.

Dead birds grew greater every day,
But mankind's greed was swift to pay,
For soon, as feared, they disappeared –
No birds flew through the sky.

Then parties searched for any few
Survivors of those flocks that flew
Across the lands in mighty bands,
A-flying through the sky.

But none did any human find,
The victims of his brutal mind.
Extinct at last – the days were past
When flocks whirred through the sky.

At Cincinnati Zoo one day,
Poor lonely Martha passed away.
The last was dead, her soul was led
Across that boundless sky.

And only then did mankind weep,
A bitter harvest would he reap
For many years, as futile tears
Fell flooding from the sky.

But though their mortal days are done,
The pigeons' spirits linger on.
For up in Space, beyond man's face,
On silent wings they fly.

Down through the ages, much has been written about the beautiful song of this close relative of the blackbird and thrush, contrasting its rich voice with its drab plumage. Here is my own homage to the nightingale, shy philomel of the night

.

The Nightingale

Drawn through the evening by strange haunting sadness
Glides a song glorious, richer than Love,
Lilting and blending in bubbling concertos,
Rising and falling, then drifting above,

Sung by a drab little minstrel of Evening,
Hidden away in the valleys of Night,
Small is his shadow, and sombre his plumage,
Soft are his feathers, and silent his flight.

Yet when his rich warbling notes ripple sweetly
Far through each woodland and dark country lane,
All stop to listen in breathtaking wonder,
'Ere this fair music grows fainter again.

Dulcet and sweet is the Song of the Evening,
Drawn from the caves of the lost and unknown,
Borne on the wing beats of swift, chilling breezes,
Past shapeless phantoms and up to the throne

Where – 'midst the Shadows of Life and Death hanging
Deep in suspensions of Time and of Space –
Night sits, serene in her mystical beauty,
Sable her image, and hidden her face.

Yet if her visage were shown for an instant,
Lit by the starlight, unveiled for a while,
We may perhaps see her wonderful beauty,
And glimpse in silence a solitary smile,

As she hears softly the Song of the Evening,
Borne from the depths of a cool country vale,
Telling of Beauty, of Love in the Highest,
Captured in song by the sweet nightingale.

Despite its small size, the praying mantis never fails to elicit within me a momentary thrill of icy shock and fear whenever I see one of these extraordinary, alienesque insects, with its mesmerising gaze and lethal pseudo-pious stance – all of which I have sought to encapsulate in the following poem.

The Praying Mantis

There it squats – Death's fearful gargoyle –
Like a monster cast from Space;
Eyes unblinking stare in silence
From its strange, hypnotic face
Like a pair of shining gemstones –
Glinting facets, cold but bright –
Gleaming softly 'midst the shadows
With a pale, unearthly light.

Here it waits amongst the leaflets
In a pious, praying stance,
Yet the burning fires of Evil
In those deathless orbs still dance
As this prayerful gorgon crouches
In an alien repose,
And its eyes, ne'er closing, flicker,
Each a fiery, blood-tipped rose.

Hush! A movement flutters downwards –
There, a small, unwary fly,
Flitting closer, ne'er perceiving
How it all too soon will die.
For within a second's lifetime,
Moving faster e'en than Thought,
Flick-knived forelegs take it captive;
And the battle has been fought.

Soon it waits again, unnoticed,
'Midst the shadows of the trees,
With intelligence so chilling
That the very sun would freeze
If this ghoul e'er gazed upon it
In the glory of the skies.
None but Death may find a shelter
In those cold, unblinking eyes.

The poetry of the mystic William Blake has enriched my life for many years, and it inspired me greatly when I sought to embody in mere words the sumptuous, passionate beauty of what must surely be the world's most alluring flower.

The Rose

Who made thee, displayed thee –
Enrapturing starlet?
A crimson inferno
'Midst flushes of scarlet.
With bright inflorescence
Like vivid fluorescence,
Who cast, ne'er surpassed thee –
Most perfect of all?

Who blessed thee, possessed thee –
Enchanting suffusion?
More lovely, more fragrant
Than any illusion.
Intensely desiring,
A lustre untiring,
Surviving and thriving
When all others fall.

Who placed thee, embraced thee
'Midst kingdoms of mortals?
Whose sunbeams caress thee
From Heaven's bright portals?
For Beauty you nourish,
And thus will you flourish
Fore'er more, until your
Creator will call.

The scientist inside my brain tells me that stars are colossal conflagrations of fiery gas burning in the depths of Outer Space untold millions of miles away, but the poet within my mind prefers to liken them to delicate flowers blooming in the evening sky overhead, or to fragile candles doomed to be extinguished by the coming of day.

The Star

Like an eye through Dark's veiled shadow
Shines a frosty-petalled star,
In a bed of hazy aura.
O'er a sleeping world afar.

Twinkling softly through the silence
Of the solitudes of Night,
Ever watching, as its fragrance
Fills the countryside with light

Like a shining flower of Heaven
From the valleys of the sky,
Till the morning's beams perceive it,
And once more doom it to die

In the burning streams of glory
From the sun's resplendent gaze,
As it wilts with lonely sadness
In a pale, pellucid haze.

But when Evening rises slowly
From the hillsides of the past,
It is born again, unblemished,
Through the dusky light to last,

Like a candle burning brightly,
Till the silhouette of Day
Spies this fragile, twilit fairy
And blows softly it away.

Surely the most spectacular sights in all of Nature are the setting and the rising of the sun, torching the skies aflame with its fiery glory as it sinks downwards to die before reappearing in resplendent triumph amid the glowing heavens.

Sunset, Sunrise

Like a golden shadow drifting
Down the corridors of Night,
Like a glowing, saffron planet
Moving past the worlds of Light,

Gliding downwards through the evening,
Past the galaxies of stars,
Past the fairy rings of Saturn,
And the burnished face of Mars.

Floating down on cloudy cushions
Hanging through the roseate skies,
Interspersed by stars that twinkle
Like a host of fireflies.

Down and down the sun sinks slowly,
To the sleeping waves and sea,
Past the shadows of the evening,
Down through all Eternity,

To the hush of bygone mornings
In the realms of dreams and sleep,
Where trees whisper through the ages,
And bright fountains softly weep,

Till the dawn with vivid brush-strokes
Paints the waking morning sky.
Then the ghosts of empty eons
Through the heavens slowly fly

In a hazy mist of star moths,
Past the mountains white with snow,
To worlds far beyond our knowing,
Where forget-me-nots still grow.

But the sun stirs slowly, gleaming
Through the drowsy clouds of grey,
Rising softly up once more, to
Greet the brimming newborn day

Like a fiery horse of Heaven,
Racing through the skies so wide.
Who would dare this steed to harness?
Who would dare the sun to ride?

What might happen if a flock of swans somehow coalesced with a herd of horses, even if only in a half-dreaming mind? That intriguing premise was the starting point for the following word-picture – a poetical flight of imagination...in every sense!

Swans and Horses

Like a phalanx borne from Heaven
On a golden drift of Love
Glides a stream of snowy shadows
From the cloud-worlds far above
In an ever-wider spiral
Sweeping slowly through the skies,
While the lake's reflection shimmers
Like a star within their eyes,
Growing brighter every second
As their silhouettes descend
To its violescent waters,
Where the ripples softly wend –
Each a trembling ring of sunlight
'Ere it falls away to die,
Just an iridescent nimbus
'Neath a cerulean sky.

Now the swans reside serenely
Near the sable-mantled shade
Of the melancholy willow
From the lakeside's dappled glade,
Where the breezy zephyr murmurs
As its gusty whispers cool
Catch the willow's pearly teardrops,
Each a tiny silvered pool
Cast in deep, despondent sorrow
As the willow bows in grief,
Dewdrops trickling down in torrents
From each slender yellow leaf.

Here the swans glide by in silence,
Necks held high in regal stance
As their eyes gaze up to Heaven
While its darting sunbeams dance
Through their incandescent plumage,
Wings held proudly o'er their back
Like an arch of sparkling crescents
Tipped with inky plumes of black.
On they glide, past ruffling meadows
Flecked with starry trains of flowers,
Blooming brightly in the shelter
Of their viridescent bowers.

And across these speckled grasslands
To the silver-spangled streams
Chase a herd of snowy horses
Like a host of starlit beams,
Manes caressed by breezy fingers,
Like a sea of moonlit waves
Surging down across their shoulders
From its underwater cave,
As their eyes, afire and glowing,
Burn with bright undying flame,
While their tails toss ever skyward
With a joy that none can tame.

Soon they pass from sight and being
'Neath the woodlands' leafy shade,
And my eyes grow weak and heavy,
Each with slumber overlaid.
Yet as Hypnos murmurs softly
From the drowsy realms of Sleep,
Still the horses race before me
As their flowing spirits leap
'Cross the streams and to the lakeside
Where the swans sedately gaze
Through the heavens' golden shadow,
Through the skies' translucent haze.

And as clouds float by in silence
O'er the warm, caressing skies,
Strange to say, the swans and horses
Merge as one before my eyes –
And as Morpheus casts softly
Dreams of slumber round my mind,
Wingèd steeds ascend to Heaven,
Leaving lake and streams behind.
Wings spread forth, and lustrous feathers
Gleam and glow like rays of light,
As these fair, enchanted visions
Pass so swiftly from my sight
To their mellow hierarchy
That no man shall ever see.
Earth is ours – a world of mortals.
Theirs is Immortality.

The spectacular, vivid spectrum of colours filling every corner of our world must surely be one of the greatest gifts that anyone can enjoy. I have always been fascinated by how this multitude of shades and hues can be expressed in words as well as by visual means, and there is surely no greater challenge than to capture and celebrate the polychromatic wonder of the rainbow within the medium of the written word. That, therefore, became my goal with this poem, to create my own vibrant multicoloured rainbow in rhyme

Through the Rainbow

Upwards I glide through a brilliant archway
Spanning the chasms of Space far above,
Sewn by the radiant needle of Heaven –
Weaving its splendour from sunbeams of Love.

Upwards and on through its crystalline crescents,
Casting a multihued shadow of Light,
Lost in a world of reflecting translucence
Showering colour in shimmering flight.

Upwards forever in vivid crescendos
Streaming like fountains through lilac-lit skies,
Swiftly ascending in bright sapphire spirals –
Sparkling like diamonds in star-showered eyes.

Upwards and onwards through whirling suffusions
Blushing like crimson-tipped roses of fire,
Passing through arches of amber and turquoise
Curving through Space like celestial lyres.

Upwards I soar through this arcuate spectrum
Spraying forth shaftlets of sun-shattered rays –
Rocketing outwards in golden aurorae
Filling the heavens with glistening haze.

Upwards, e'er upwards, like amethyst arrows
Bursting asunder with petals of flame,
Riding forever the arcs of the rainbow;
Light is my spirit, and Colour my name.

Tigers have always fascinated me, but I was only too aware that any attempt to capture this great cat's beauty and power in verse would be fraught with the peril of comparison with William Blake's spellbinding 'Tyger Tyger'. Nevertheless, eventually the lure of challenge became too great, and the following poem is my own tribute to this most magnificent, and terrifying, of creatures.

The Tiger

Deep in the primeval fires of the cosmos
Death was released from his shimmering tomb,
And as they danced in the dawn of Creation
Death bore a child from the flames of their womb.

You were that child, spawned by Death's great Inferno,
Hidden on Earth 'neath his Shadow of Fear,
Shrouded by Night until Heaven sent sunlight,
Then, by its silhouette, did you appear.

Who could have known that such beauty held terror
Deep within radiant emerald eyes,
Wrought and emblazoned in Death's blazing furnace,
Dewdrops of fear like the tears that you cry?

Space cannot hold you, and Time dare not chain you,
None can oppose you in glittering might.
Ebony ripples lash amber resplendence,
Scorning the shame of the sun's feeble light,

Scorching through Night like a firebrand of crimson,
Shredding the skies with each thunderous breath.
Yet, though so splendorous, e'er are you deadly,
Chilling in form, for your beauty is Death.

Who hasn't stared up at the sky, and in their imagination transformed the clouds floating by into all manner of images – dragons, horses, faces, and countless other forms? Sometimes, however, clouds remind me of ghosts – silent phantoms stealing across an empty stage before vanishing from sight.

Watching the Clouds

Silver ghosts of silent skies,
Moving softly, phantomwise,
Through the planes of wind and space,
Freckles on the sky's blue face.

Snowy-white in weightless ease,
On they float o'er lands and seas,
Through the realms of Space and Time,
Past dark lands and worlds sublime.

Changing shape and size they sail,
Leaving neither path nor trail,
Moving onwards, roaming free,
Through unseen Eternity.

And when Evening draws its veil
'Cross the globe, still on they sail,
Round the sun as down it sinks;
Now they're mauve, and flushed with pink.

So they leave, with tips of fire,
Over seas of bright sapphire,
Darkened now till Dawn's release,
Downy clouds on wings of Peace.

PART 2:
OTHER WORLDS

There are other worlds everywhere – worlds of Space and Time, mirror worlds and shadow worlds, worlds of sleep and starlight, fire and phantoms, snowfall and death, and the myriad inner worlds of the imagination. Journey with me now into some of my own worlds, far from those of the dreary waking day.

To see a world in a grain of sand
And a heaven in a wild flower,
Hold Infinity in the palm of your hand
And Eternity in an hour.

William Blake – 'To See a World'

All of us beings here are cells of the unknown essence of our world, nodes of flesh that could as well be notes of melody. We are part of something infinite and eternal. There is no boundary between us and the world. In a profoundly relative sense, each of us may simultaneously occupy that particular focal point through which the entire universe is singing at this moment.

Are we then God's dream set to music in the place where the sea and the wind have begun to awake and think? Grateful for our blessing, even when they hurt, we trust the world is not paining needlessly for our sweet incertitudes 'twixt desire and reason. We would wish to be wiser and more loving, but for good or ill, our memories are young in this ancient oasis. And we comprehend little. How indeed could a part hear the Whole, or a note the Melody?

Yet the silence of space that enwombs the earth is not totally void. Indeed it is now revealed to be latent, pregnant, mystic — even as it was in the beginning that had no beginning — even as it will be in the end that can have no end. For this is the secret of the spirit that is the life of the form that is the language of the spirit — the eternal spirit that somewhere, somehow, found its voice, took wing and came alive.

Guy Murchie – *The Seven Mysteries of Life*

This poem was penned by me as an exercise in personification, imagining all of the major elements – the dawn (Eos), sky, sun, moon, stars, evening, sleep, and day – as living entities, making their entrances and exits in Shakespearean grandeur upon the ultimate stage, Heaven

The Awakening of Day

Silently, Eos rekindles her candle,
Sending forth slowly each flickering ray,
Snaring the stars as they twinkle in slumber –
Caught unaware by the heralds of Day.

And as the sky draws its shimmering curtain
Back 'cross the dark, empty windows of Night,
Swiftly the sun casts its soft, cloudy blankets
Far through the heavens in ripples of light,

Yawning, as Sleep glides unseen from his bedside
Back to her valley of wandering dreams,
Then rising proudly through radiant Heaven,
Painting the morning with glistening beams,

Showering all with a fountain of sunlight,
All but the moon draped in shadows of grey,
Silently mourning the exile of Evening –
Banished from Space by the coming of Day.

Bidding farewell, like a frail agèd spinster,
Leaving at last her celestial home,
Passes the moon 'cross the heavens' bright archway,
Ending beneath Twilight's crystalline dome.

There she will rest, till the sun's golden shadow
Drips from the sky in a puddle of grey.
Then like a ghost will the moon rise in glory,
Called into life by the cortège of Day.

I wrote this poem as a paean of praise to Nature – and, indeed, to Supernature, even Ultranature, perfect Nature beyond humanity's normal sensory perceptions – and to its glory through all eternity, as personified by Perpetua.

Dreams of Nature

Through sleepy vales of pastel green
I passed, one Summer morning;
'Neath dreaming skies of blissful blue
Reborn with Daylight's dawning,
While faraway the ocean's roars
Still echoed long from silent shores.

And on I strolled, 'neath golden clouds,
Past dancing, crystal fountains
That leapt and sang in sparkling joy
From lilac, snow-capped mountains
Like diamond stars with lucent glee,
And blessed by Immortality.

And through the skies the sun was drawn
By two emblazoned horses
That raced along a burnished trail –
Two crimson, fiery forces
With streaming tails like scarlet lyres,
And scorching eyes like dancing fires.

Still on I passed through glades of trees –
Tall, silver dendroids gleaming
Like astral arcs with spangled boughs,
And fragrant flowers beaming,
Pulsating light in fragile streams
Like cloudy, half-forgotten dreams.

Ah, Nature! Truly thou art here,
Amidst thine own perfection,
In this, thy world of unborn dreams,
For who could give correction
To this, thy realm, and thine alone,
Which Time's own seeds could not have sown.

And meadows flecked with sleeping flowers
Lay far into the distance –
For Nature gave them love of Life,
The will for their existence –
Exuding sweet, enchanting scent
That zephyrs' drifting murmurs sent

Across the cerulean hills
To kiss the mauve reflections
Of pool and lake in lilac groves,
Translucent, clear perfections,
Each rippling long, with violet torqued,
As turquoise swallows skimmed and hawked.

And here I see thou dwellest too,
Perpetua, my dearest,
Whose eyes reflect the vales of Space
Like pools of beauty clearest.
For here thou too can seek release,
For here alone thou findest Peace.

Ah, Peace! I see thy figure bright –
A slender, tranquil maiden
Amidst the elvish vales and woods,
All intricately laden
With gauzy webs of spider-thread
In rippling green and blushing red.

So look into the western skies
And see her shadow shining –
A smiling face with deep blue eyes
As pure as Heaven's lining.
And there, amid the clouds above,
A Sign is born – a snowy Dove.

Perpetua – all knowest thee –
Celestial, immortal –
Who passes e'er through Space's door,
Through Time's eternal portal,
To other worlds concealed from all,
Till all receive the Shining Call.

And from the rainbow's golden end
The souls of Colour fluttered
In evanescent cloudy drifts,
As ageless mountains muttered
'Neath shattered brows of crumbling stone,
As old and pale as whitened bone.

And all around lies Space, supreme –
A vacuum dark, unending –
Which bore thee once, Perpetua,
To send thy spirit wending
From wells of Time to strange new worlds
Where dormant Life would be unfurled.

And so, as star steeds raced in joy
Across their twinkling haven,
I took my leave of Nature's bliss
'Neath darkened mountains graven.
For Time is swifter still, it seems,
And past are all my Nature dreams.

For now I wake, once more alone
Amidst my own surrounding.
Yet still within my sleepy eyes
The star steeds' souls are bounding.
And still, Perpetua, I see
Thee shining far ahead of me.

Yea, ever will I see thy face
Before my life's ambition,
As e'er wilt thou personify
My lifetime's expedition,
Till I no more this world shall see,
For, yea, thou art Eternity.

Who hasn't stared into the bright flickering flames of a fire and imagined all manner of ever-changing sights portrayed by their savage yet beautiful dance?

Fire Pictures

Amid the fire's auroral glow
Lie far-off realms of long ago,
Recaptured now in crimson hues
With violet tints and smoky blues.

Imagination often takes
My searching eyes past amber lakes
Where groves of scarlet forests sway
'Midst scorching, incandescent rays.

And golden steeds with flaming manes
Race endlessly o'er burnished plains,
While hidden 'neath the fiery skies
Prowl lions bold, with ruby eyes.

And conflagrating dragons roar,
While streaming bolts of lightning pour
From seething nostrils, tongue, and heart,
And from their jaws flames curl and dart.

Emblazoned chateaux rise through clouds
'Midst burning willows downward-bowed,
And through the coruscating skies
The iridescent phoenix flies.

But soon, before my dazzled eyes,
Each splendid vision fades and dies,
Until no flame eruptions spout;
For all is gone – the fire is out.

Yet hidden from my silent eyes,
Like unseen candles through the skies,
The souls of Fire flit on in Space
To other worlds beyond my face.

And there, perhaps, another child
Will witness their enchantment wild,
And see himself, in flickers curled,
The mystic lands of Fire unfurled.

When writing, I often find myself returning to certain themes and motifs – mirrors and reflections, shadows and phantoms, parallel worlds, the past and future uniting, solitude, silence, and God. All of these, and more, can be found here.

The Ghost

Who stands 'neath the eaves draped in shadows?
Who dwells 'midst the darkness of Night?
Who calls with a whisper of pathos,
In sorrowful, meaningless flight?

"I stand – 'midst the dusk of the evening;
I call – from the far side of Time;
I flit – 'midst the valleys of Sadness,
Rhyme lacking in reasonless rhyme.

"I call – I alone, I unnoticed
In Morning's pale sun-shadowed dawn.
I call – from the noontide's bright wonder,
As I through all kingdoms am borne.

"I dwell 'midst a grey world of Shadow
E'erlasting, past all mortal sight –
A parallel world, silhouetted
In pools' depthless doorways of Light.

"And here you may see me reflected –
A phantom transparent in Space.
And in your eyes, Memory-painted,
Look inward to witness my face –

"A face from the Past and the Future,
Recaptured and borne into being –
A shadow – till stand I unblemished,
An infant before the All-Seeing."

Our innermost emotions can assume many forms, but, hopefully, none as tangibly malevolent as the version described here – ophiophobes, look away now!

Green Snake

Well I know you, gleaming Green Snake,
Brightly wrapped in shining mail.
Well I know your silent movement,
Gliding forth on glinting scales,

To your unsuspecting victim
Sleeping peacefully in bed,
As your forked tongue whispers softly
Through the dreams that fill his head.

Now your coils enfold him tightly
In a feverish embrace,
And a potent stream of venom
Drips like fire upon his face

As your toxic tongue still murmurs
Like a wind through silent leaves,
Infiltrating his subconscious,
Till inside his mind it weaves

Webs of Doubt and Greed and Envy,
Soon eclipsing Love and Bliss,
Turning Beauty into Hatred –
Strong and deadly is your kiss.

And when morning comes, your victim
Rises full of Rage and Spite,
Hurting others with his cruelty,
Setting Love and Peace alight

By the flame of Hate inside him
That one day, his heart, will take.
Yes, I know you well of old – for
You are Jealousy, Green Snake.

In Greek mythology, Mnemosyne was the mother of the nine Muses, and was also the personification of memory. But just how accurate, how reliable, are our memories? For when we look back at our life, how much of what we remember is real, and how much is what we'd have liked it to have been?

The Mirror of Mnemosyne

Dark, still, enshadowed, the mirror of Mnemosyne,
Moonlight encircling its chill, quicksilvered face.
Standing beside it, the masked goddess of Memory,
Ageless, all-seeing, transcending time and space.

Dare for a moment to gaze into her looking-glass,
See what you may in its crystalline mirage,
Brimming with happiness, hope, despair, and tragedy,
Each mood reflected upon its pale visage.

Do not anticipate viewing your own imagery,
Nor will your past be recaptured and displayed.
All you will see is the sum of your remembrances,
Rose-tinged distortions, each summoned and replayed.

These are your yesterdays, edited and modified,
Transformed by memory, shaped and cast anew.
Now just as real as the past itself had ever been,
Dreams become history, tangible and true.

So, as you linger, your captive eyes still mesmerised,
Drawn through the depths of the mirror's sable pool,
Who can be sure that the past is not a fantasy,
Mocking our minds like the laughter of a fool?

The following poem owes its creation to a very curious snatch of conversation that I happened by chance to overhear one day on the radio, in which the speaker was contemplating whether it might be that many of the people that we casually pass by without interaction or see only from a distance are nothing more than ghosts, mere phantoms. And so, from this remarkable muse, sprang 'A Phantasia' (constituting, incidentally, the longest single sentence to appear in any of my writings!).

A Phantasia of Ghosts and Illusions

Hear the echo of a lifetime
Doomed forever more to last,
Or a murmur drifting backwards
From the theatres of the past,

Whirling softly through a vortex
Spinning deep in silent Space
Like a whirlpool in the heavens,
Or an eye within a face

Gazing outwards, yet unseeing,
Pale as Dawn's auroral birth
From the snowy dreams of slumber
Shrouding velvet, verdant Earth,

Like an unseen clock vibrating
As its lifetime ebbs away,
While its fingers trace the seconds
Of another unborn day

Through the silhouettes cast downwards
From the shadows of the stars,
Now a host of winging phantoms
From a distant world afar,

Flitting slowly through the evening
As the planets e'er rotate,
Each a windmill in a spiral
On a shining, spangled plate

Spinning outwards e'er to nowhere
In their orbit round their lord,
While lugubrious crescendos
Chase like half-forgotten chords

In a lonely helter-skelter
Through the avenues of Time;
They – the spheres' eternal music –
Lacking syllables or rhyme,

Drifting downwards through the starlight
Lest their meaning fades away
To a ghost upon the moorlands
Of an evanescent day

Ever seeking 'midst the future
For a future of its own,
As the souls of Past and Present
Soar like cloudlets to the throne

Of a duplicated kingdom
On Time's unknown, farthest side,
Where their memory still lingers,
Round its universe to glide,

While they merge with more illusions –
None is real, for none can be
In this pseudo-world of Shadow
Cast from vacant Destiny

Like a set of footprints chasing
After footprints of their own,
Or a pool's encircling ripples
Running rings around a stone;

Yet their messengers are present
In a hundred other lands,
Groping ever through their darkness
Like a metamorphic hand,

E'en within our crowded suburbs
'Midst their noisy, raucous hosts,
Who could guess that most are shadows,
Mindless images, just ghosts?

Mirrors have always fascinated me, confronting me with my other self, exact but reversed, and showing me a glimpse of their replicate world – as real as my own, and, who knows, perhaps even more so?

Reflections in the Mirror

I am me, and you are also.
Am I you, or are you me,
As we gaze, each seeming brighter,
Into deep Eternity?

And your mirror world shines softly
With a cool quicksilver light
As your searching eyes call ever
For my spirit's silent flight

Through the mirror's timeless border
To the other side of Space,
Where my world is yours reflected
In the mirror's glossy face.

All stands still in ageless wonder
As my world just flutters by
Like a phantom caught by daylight
In the glowing eastern sky.

But I enter not this kingdom –
The inversion of my own.
Yet I stand before the mirror
Like an image lost, alone,

And my other calls me softly
Through the mirror's sparkling hue
As I gaze, and still I wonder,
Are you me, or am I you?

What happens to our shadow when we sleep? Does it lie hidden amid the darkness of other shadows, awaiting our awakening, or does it depart for adventures of its own amid Night's secret dominions? Ever since I first read Hans Christian Andersen's enthralling but chilling story, 'The Shadow' as a youngster, I have always been intrigued, and possibly even a little troubled, by that niggling thought.

The Shadow

Here I walk and you walk also,
Long you've travelled by my side,
Dark and mystical as Evening,
Through whose cryptic lands you glide

When I slip in silent slumber
From your world of starlit Night.
Then you too, in unseen swiftness,
Travel far in darkened flight

To the sombre Night-time nations,
Past each moonlit tree and glade,
Where the veiled domains of Evening
To your form become displayed,

As you pass by lonely islets
In the seas of Dark and Gloom,
While the misty ghosts of Evening
Through the sable valleys loom.

For your world lies deeply hidden
From the sunlight's dancing beams,
In the phantom realms of Evening,
And the secret world of Dreams.

I am Light, and you are Darkness;
I am Day, and you are Night.
Yet remain we close together,
Still within each other's sight;

And will be, until my leaving
For another World afar.
Then beyond my sight you'll vanish,
'Neath the shadow of the stars.

Much has been written about the scientific and philosophical associations between sleep and death, but the ancient Greeks encapsulated these links in a particularly telling, succinct manner via personification. For in classic Greek mythology, death is a god called Thanatos (not to be confused, though he often is, with Hades, god of the Underworld), and is the twin brother of Hypnos, god of sleep, with Morpheus, god of dreams, as the son of Hypnos. Moreover, the parents of Thanatos and Hypnos are none other than Nyx (Night) and Erebos (Darkness). In addition, one of the most famous death-related scenes in Greek mythology is the passage across the River Styx to the Underworld of the boat steered by Charon the silent ferryman and filled with the souls of the dead. Consequently, to emphasise the ancient Greeks' perceived kinship between death and sleep, I chose to adapt the latter boat scene, transforming it from one that features the dead to an equivalent featuring sleepers and sleep (though as a female rather than male personification), but acknowledging the link between sleep and death by way of the final verse.

Sleep

Day sinks away through the oceans of Evening,
Rippling like stars sweeping outwards to die,
While from their vortex the moon rises softly,
Borne from its depths to the roof of the sky.

And 'cross the waters a boat glides serenely,
Nod is its helmsman, and Sleep is its queen.
Gently it drifts o'er the waves deep in slumber,
Dappled in shadows of violet and green.

Grey are the sails, each dream-woven by Twilight,
Sewn from the cobwebs that Morning passed by;
Pale is its image 'neath moonlit aurorae,
Fashioned from memories, murmurs, and sighs.

And from its silhouette Sleep whispers gently,
Calling to mortals who follow like shades –
Entering slowly her boat of enchantment,
Drawn through the evening to mystical glades

Deep in the depths of the hidden subconscious,
'Neath the dark heavens of shimmering Night –
Silently watching her star-shadowed journey
Into the morning, 'ere fading from sight.

Waves bear Sleep calmly through dream-clouded kingdoms,
Misty surroundings of lilac and grey,
Fragile illusions like butterfly wing beats,
Melting like ghosts 'neath the lantern of Day.

And as the dawn blushes shyly through Heaven,
Far 'cross the ocean is Sleep softly borne,
Each mortal soul drifting back to its dwelling,
Waking once more to the laughter of Morn.

Thus she continues – the wisest immortal –
Fair both in features and mind she'll remain,
Leading our souls till the world calls no longer,
Then shall we never look homeward again.

One of the most mesmerising figures in fantasy literature must surely be the Snow Queen as conceived by Hans Christian Andersen. Here is my tribute to the alluring, illusive kingdom of snow and its bewitching, pitiless monarch.

Snow Dreaming

A wilderness, white and unending,
Lay waiting, my soul to enfold,
As softly its slim, chilling fingers
Froze even my whispers with cold.

Its shimmering mantle draped slowly
My ankles with starflakes of snow,
While winds from the chateaux of Winter
Sent billowing murmurs of woe

Through clouds each suspended from Heaven
O'er landscapes enveloped in white,
As faintly a polar sun flickered –
A candle of shivering light.

And ever the icicles glittered,
Like pendants transparent and cool,
And ever the visage of Winter
Laughed softly through crystalline pools,

While snowflakes drew pale, bitter petals
O'er window, and garden, and door,
As slowly my steps led me onwards,
But only a nothingness saw.

For grimly the blizzard lashed downwards –
A phantom as chilling as Death –
As ever I strove to avoid it,
To turn from its glacial breath.

But Winter's pale wraiths sang out softly,
And slowly their song drew me on,
Till, howling, the winds quelled their music,
And when I looked up, they were gone.

Yet there, in their stead, just beyond me,
The Snow Queen stood, calling my name.
To struggle was futile, was useless,
As ever approaching she came.

Her arms stretched out glowing towards me,
Enticing me nearer to Doom,
As, frozen, my spirit lay dormant –
A ghost in a windowless room.

Her eyes laughed in terrible silence,
Cold diamonds of shimmering blue.
And closer I stumbled towards her,
As stronger her influence grew,

Till spectres of snow loomed all round me
Like phantasms shapeless and pale,
Enshrouded in misty grey mantles,
And spangled with gemstones of hail.

Then softly a Voice spoke beyond them:
"Walk on – to your world, and your home."
The sun shone forth strongly above me,
A beacon from Heaven's bright dome.

And when I looked onwards, the Snow Queen
Grew wan in the sun's holy light
Until, like a great mournful shadow,
Her form passed away from my sight.

And silence once more lay behind me,
Retracing my vanishing track.
And ever the sun led me onwards.
And nothing again called me back.

Here is a word-picture poem revealing a silver-hued fantasy realm of starlight, far removed in space and time from our own mundane world. So let your imagination take wing for a while, and leave the cares of our sad little planet far behind.

Starlight Fantasia

Like a sphere of icy moonlight,
Like a spool of shrouded snow,
Lies a world in sparkling starlight,
Turning softly, far below,

In its orbit through the heavens,
Gliding on as e'er it moves
Round its sleepy sun in wonder,
Drawn through unseen astral grooves.

Birds more lovely than a rainbow
Dart beneath its shadowed trees,
And the sylphs with gauzy mantles
Float upon the evening breeze.

And throughout the misty heavens
Swans and horses swiftly fly,
Down beneath the dappling moonbeams
Where the planets journey by.

And the mottled trees of night-time
Whisper melodies of grace,
But their songs are those of ages,
Spanning lifetimes, worlds, and Space.

Silver pools of starlit sadness
Ripple on through countless hours,
While soft music rises upwards
From the evening's blooming flowers –

Calling through the planes of stardust,
Through a universe of stars,
Answered by a thousand minstrels
From another world afar.

Sapphire swallow calls to swallow
O'er the spider-webs of Time,
And a hundred thousand bluebirds
Sing with dulcet tones sublime.

Still the planets circle softly
'Midst the sable cloak of Night,
Calling softly, ever calling,
Through the shimmering starlight,

Like a thousand ghostly murmurs,
Like a hundred ringing chimes,
Like great butterflies they move through
Silent corridors of Time.

Only they have learnt the secret
That no thing is what it seems,
Just illusions, simply shadows,
In an everlasting dream.

And when Dawn arises slowly
Out of Evening's cavern deep,
Mystery flies softly westward
To the spiralled realms of Sleep.

And when we slowly awaken,
We know not of what is past,
Of the haunting worlds behind us,
Which forever more will last,

Till the shining, gleaming planets,
Softly dying, fade to grey.
And then we will know their secret,
As we slowly fly away.

Two very different poems of mine owe their origin to an extraordinary, surreal painting by René Magritte. Entitled 'The Voice of the Winds', it depicts three enormous, alien-looking spheres floating ominously above a rural scene. Whereas one of my poems, 'The Music of the Spheres' (included in Part 5 of this present collection), was directly influenced by that compelling image, the other poem, presented below, focuses instead upon the painting's very evocative title.

The Voice of the Winds

Dark the forest lay, silent and sombre,
In Morning's first saffron-lit rays,
As the trees swayed, each shrouded in shadows
Of glimmering ochres and greys.

But the sun rose up higher through Heaven,
And splashes of sunlight appeared
Through the leaflets of trees overlapping,
As Morning through rosy skies peered.

And amidst shady groves I stood, dappled
With silhouettes cast from above,
While the dewdrops hung round me like crystals,
As soft as the tears from a dove,

Each inverting and changing its image,
Distorting the forest and trees.
And the Voice of the Winds called me forwards,
Borne swiftly on Morning's light breeze.

And I followed, to see through the clearing,
The forest pool, glassy and bright;
Its calm surface in clear violescence
Reflecting the dawn's filtered light.

Swirling ripples raced madly in circles,
Increasing, till, skimming from view,
More appeared from the central gyration,
Each polychromatic in hue.

And I yearned for the pool to caress me,
As I on the bankside stood long.
And the Voice of the Winds called me onwards
In lyrical segments of song.

So I entered, and felt the pool's wonder
Embrace me in eager repose.
And I gazed through its glistening beauty,
As o'er me its silhouette rose.

Here I stood 'midst its clear undulations,
And Weight left my beckoning soul.
Now the world lay below me in silence –
A solitary, orbiting bowl.

And I stood in this limitless limbo,
Where all was a daydream sublime,
And the Voice of the Winds called me upwards,
To Doorways of Heaven, and Time.

I have always harboured a somewhat Quixotic captivation for windmills, and this following poem was inspired by the very eyecatching cover of a 1970s record album that featured a spectacular, multicoloured image of a windmill created by time-lapse photography, in which its arms seemed to be turning not merely through the air but also through space and even through time itself.

The Windmill

Like an astral wheel of Heaven
Sweeping silently through Space,
Never ceasing, never easing
In its convoluted pace,

Like an outward-coiling spiral
As its spool spins ever on
Through the webs of Space forever
Till its silhouette has gone,

Past the stars all draped in wonder
As its whirling arms sweep down
Through the solitudes of darkness
In the evening's velvet gown.

Still its shadow keeps on turning
Past the zenith of the skies,
For the windmill's winding pivot
Is where Time most surely lies,

E'er gyrating on its axis
Like a pendulum in Space,
As through depthless pools and chasms
Its unwinding fingers trace –

Like a clock revolving slowly,
Lacking rhythm, lacking rhyme,
Just rotating through the heavens
As the centre-stone of Time.

Imagine a multicoloured flight of winged Faerie folk, flitting swiftly from their hidden world through the realms of dreams to greet the dawning day, then on through forgotten lands of shadow until night appears, whereupon they return at last to their own secret world. That's what I did – and this poem was the result.

Worlds of Faerie

Small songbirds sing and bluebells ring,
And Faerie folk fly through the sky.
Red, blue, and green, yet never seen,
For on swift wings they softly fly.
Past rainbow arcs, like shining larks
They flit through unseen Faerie lands,
Through clouds of blue with violet hue,
To silent seas with silver sands.

Here, waves of dreams flow on in streams
To sleepy shores where moonlight shines.
Then on they fly through silken sky,
To elvish realms where shadows line
Each dawning day, as sunlit fays
Draw golden trains across the skies.
Still on they speed, where sunlight leads
To lands forgotten, draped in sighs
Of clouded grey, which overlay
These worlds with hazy mists of gloom.
Where nothing's real, as phantoms steal
Across their lands and on to doom.

But fairies turn where sunlight burns
Down warm upon the countryside.
Then Night draws near, so on they steer
To fairy groves, in which they glide,
Away from eyes that seek to pry
Into the secrets of their world,
Which stays apart from human hearts
Until, to Time, is all unfurled.

PART 3:
A SENSE OF MYSTERY

Even as a child, the ordinary world was never enough for me – I was always irresistibly attracted to everything that was extraordinary, mysterious, fabulous, unexpected (making my interest in cryptozoology, for instance, an inevitability). Consequently, it should come as no surprise to discover that such themes have inspired many of my poems too, as revealed in the following selection.

If, when hearing that I have been stilled at last, they stand at the door,
Watching the full-starred heavens that winter sees,
Will this thought rise on those who will meet my face no more,
"He was one who had an eye for such mysteries"?

Thomas Hardy – 'Afterwards'

Dark, black giant butterflies
kill the radiance of the sun.
And earthwards from the sky
the monsters invisible,
with heavy pinions, sink
down upon the hearts of men.

Albert Giraud – 'Night', in *Pierrot Lunaire*

When the evening wind blusters lustily through the willows, are they merely being blown from side to side in passive defeat, or could it be that they are dancing in moonlit wistfulness, unseen by the sleeping eyes of mankind as they perform their graceful ballet and murmur sad melodies beneath a bright panoply of stars?

Ballet of the Willows

Softly the moon glides in cloud-cushioned orbit
Far through the star-sequined shades of the skies,
Wafting through Space like a shimmering teardrop
Silently falling from Night's velvet eyes.
And as the stars blink through lavender curtains,
Twinkling their heavenly lanterns of light,
Nightingale rhapsodies sail through the woodlands,
Sweet dulcet music to serenade Night,

Drifting 'cross lakesides where willows sway gently –
Boughs kissed by starlight as downwards they bend,
Arching, as crescents of silver-shot rainbows
Dance through their branches, while moon shaftlets wend
Downwards to die in the willows' reflection –
Trapped like a thought in the mirrors of Space –
Fading from sight as the willows' soft murmurs
Ripple and rise o'er the lake's silver face,

Whispering gently in long chords of sadness
Dreams from the very beginning of time,
Singing in voices each soft yet unending,
Hauntingly wistful yet strangely sublime,
Swaying in dance as the swift evening breezes
Spiral and curl through their emerald leaves,
Combing them gently with cool twilit fingers,
Stroking each softly as round them they weave,

Silently laughing like souls of the evening,
Mournfully sighing like ghosts of the dawn,
Leaving at last as the sun rises slowly,
Borne on the wings of the first breath of morn.
And as the sun paints its glorious murals
Far 'cross the heavens in burnishing hue,
Silent and still are the tall golden willows,
Each weeping diamonds of glittering dew.

Yet, far above them, through vast cloudy strata,
Still their soft voices soar upwards and on.
E'er will they sing in the vales of the future,
E'en when the whispering willows have gone,
E'en when their lakeside reflection has faded –
Melting like gold 'neath the sun's crimson face –
Ne'er more to snare their ethereal beauty,
Lost like a dream in the cobwebs of Space.

Fantasy horses – such as unicorns, flying horses, and star steeds – have always held a particular fascination for me, as will be revealed in this section. So here is the first of several variations upon this exotic equine theme – the thunder horse, which features in the traditional legends of North America's Sioux tribe. Interestingly, during the 19th Century the Sioux showed various scientists some huge bones said to be from thunder horses, and when these were examined they were found to be the fossilised remains of a hitherto-undescribed form of gigantic prehistoric mammal distantly related to rhinoceroses, which scientists duly christened Brontotherium – *the thunder beast.*

Behold the Thunder Horse

Dark lie the skies, as an ebony ocean
Rippling with cloudlets of surf-showered foam,
Lashed by the whipcords of storm-harnessed lightning,
Raking the heavens with fiery combs,

Savagely striking like flame-spitting cobras
Flicking their tongues through the vapours of Night,
Streaking through Space like a phalanx of dragons –
Melting the candlewax stars in their flight.

And as the skies part their dark, scorching curtains
Lit by the flickering shadows of fire,
Out from the flames rears a black steed of thunder,
Phoenix-wise born from a burnishing pyre –

Eyes blazing fiercely like crimson infernos,
Flashing like meteors bolting through Space,
Flames roaring loudly through dark velvet nostrils,
Framing with fire his illustrious face –

Streaming to Earth like a star cast from Heaven,
Wingtips alight with vermillion plumes,
Tail tossing high, now a flickering candle
Burning a trail through the smouldering gloom.

And as he lands on a grey, brooding mountain,
Mane ruffling far like a meadow of fire,
Thunder is borne from his deafening hoof-beats,
Echoing far like a vast booming choir.

Clashing in Space, these celestial cymbals
Loudly resound through the battle-torn skies,
Shredded and shattered by arrows of lightning
Shooting like flames from the thunder gods' eyes –

Gazing to Earth as their mighty steed races
Far 'cross the mountains in glorious flight,
Hooves ringing far, as the star on his forehead
Slashes the heavens with sabres of light.

Onward he surges, through hillside and valley,
Singeing the treetops with each fiery roar,
Vomiting flames like a spurting volcano
Booming with menace from skyline to shore.

Yet as he glows like a lava-lit furnace
Far through the sequin-sewn shades of the night,
Evening flits softly from purple-hued heavens,
Bidding farewell as she passes from sight,

Leaving the skies now as slumbering Morning
Shakes off her rose-petal blankets of sleep,
Soon to ascend through the clouds, soft and fleecy –
Frolicking gaily like clusters of sheep –

Bearing the sun like a glistening globule
Dripping its molten aurorae through Space,
Hanging it deftly from Heaven's bright archway,
Lighting in splendour her shimmering face.

And as she smiles in the sun's golden mirror,
Thunderclouds wilt, sinking downwards to die,
Blown from the heavens by Morning's gay laughter,
Nothing remains but a soft lonely sigh.

Now, far below, like an ebony shadow,
Rising on pinions emblazoned with fire,
Swiftly their stallion soars through the heavens,
Upwards once more to his ultimate pyre,

Swiftly approaching the sun's bright corona –
Hung like a burnishing nimbus in Space –
Nearer and nearer, till wingtip and halo
Melt into one 'midst the heaven's warm face.

Gone is the steed of the storm cloud and thunder –
Far past the dawn's bright eruption of light –
Lost in the radiant sun's incandescence
Borne through the clouds in its luminous flight.

Yet if the thunder gods e'er should roar loudly
Far through the heavens of some future night,
Then would he rise in a great conflagration,
Streaming on pinions of flame-feathered light,

Scorching through Space like a blazing colossus,
Tail curving high like a smouldering lyre,
Spraying with flames this caliginous shadow –
Borne into life by the spirit of fire.

When I wrote this poem during the 1970s, the threat of nuclear devastation was uppermost in many people's minds, with the bombing of Hiroshima and Nagasaki a mere three decades earlier. Another four decades have now passed, and, with them, I pray, the danger that these verses' dread scenario might one day come to pass.

The Bomb

Like an incandescent mushroom
Rising slowly through the skies,
As its image heaves and billows
In a shadowed cloak of sighs.

Thus it grows, a mournful spectre
From a silent world of gloom,
As it surges up, still watching
O'er a dead, forgotten tomb.

Clouds of darkness hang, suspended
From its parapet of death.
All have felt the bitter lustre
Of its all-consuming breath.

And below, a final mutant
Writhes in silence, pale and wan,
For his form is undistinguished,
Yet this creature once was Man –

At the feet of his creation,
Now released to enter Space,
Laughing inwardly in silence
As its dark, despairing face

Gazes down to watch its maker,
Left to shrink in fear and cry
'Neath a choking veil of vapour
'Ere he crawls away to die.

Now the shadow rises upwards,
For its work has been fulfilled.
Just like all, it had a purpose
That the Shining One had willed.

Radiation's shrouded Doorway
Had been opened to the world.
If Man could have only known that
Death himself had been unfurled.

Surrounded by her minions of many kinds, the Fairy Queen slumbers peacefully through the starlit wonder of a summer's night, guarded from prying eyes, and lulled by the nightingale's lilting song...

Fairy Lullaby

Speak not near our Fairy Queen, you spotted snakes and warty toads;
Fly not near our Fairy Queen, you wingèd bats of fields and roads.
Bring her peace this summer night, and let sweet scent fill air and space,
Charming Sleep to bring her slumber as the moon shines o'er her face.

Philomel, with sweet enchantment, sing to her your song of Night,
While the moon moves through the heavens in its pale, bewitching flight,
Like a pool of dreams and lullabies whose notes drift down to Earth,
Borne on wings of silver moonlight that to Mystery gave birth.

Spiders small, with spots of stardust twinkling softly in the night,
Draw not near our Fairy Queen as on your webs you race in flight;
Shining beetles, black and armoured, scuttle far from fairy eyes,
Or King Oberon's great chariot you'll draw through evening skies.

Till the rosy dawn arises from the snowy clouds of Sleep,
May you rest in worlds beyond us, in a slumber warm and deep.
And when Morning has appeared, then may you wake and fly away,
In your carriage drawn by butterflies, to greet the newborn day.

One of the most exquisite examples of cinematic animation that I have ever seen is contained within the 'Pastoral Symphony' segment of Walt Disney's animated masterpiece 'Fantasia', and features a phalanx of flying horses spiralling downwards from the sky to settle gracefully upon the surface of a sparkling blue lake. The following poem is my word-picture homage to that breathtakingly beautiful scene.

Flying Horse Fantasia

From the heavens' rainbowed archways
To the clear blue lake below
Soars a flock of flying horses,
Down and down, where rivers flow
Round the willows and the fountains,
Past the sparkling waterfalls,
To the mountains and the valleys,
Where lone Echo softly calls.

Down and down they swoop in glory,
Flowing manes and silver tails,
Through the lilac clouds of Summer,
Over meadowlands and vales.
Round they circle, wheeling swiftly
In a graceful sweeping flight,
As the sky pours forth its tribute
In a shower of golden light.

Down they glide towards the water
As their wondrous wings surge round.
Then alighting on the surface,
They fold back without a sound,
As these equine swans of Summer
Drift across the azure lake,
Heads held high in noble splendour,
Pinions trailing in their wake.

Blossom swirls upon the waters
Like a host of golden charms,
While the air is filled with singing,
And the sound of murmured psalms.
Then the wingèd colts neigh loudly
As their graceful parents glide
Far across the lustrous waters
To the lake's far-distant side.

Both as regal as the sunset,
One as snowy as a dove,
And the other, black as Midnight,
Each with eyes so full of love,
As they call in dulcet voices
To their boisterous colts behind,
Shining blue, and pink, and lemon,
Flowing manes all intertwined.

And as Morning's sunlight shimmers
On the waters' mirror bright,
It reflects five flying horses
Soaring slowly out of sight,
Past the golden drifts of sunbeams,
And the shadows of the morn,
To idyllic lands beyond them
In a pastel-shaded dawn.

When I was younger, my grandmother, Mrs Gertrude Timmins, told me of how, one evening many years earlier, she and other members of her family had stood in her bedroom watching three brightly-coloured UFOs circling back and forth for quite a while in the skies above their home in the town of Wednesbury, in the West Midlands, England, before eventually flying away, never to return. Not having seen a UFO, I had to content myself by imagining how it might be if I ever did do so.

The Flying Saucer

Through the night-time's spangled valleys
My enquiring eyes raced far,
Still enchanted by the beauty
Of each twinkling evening star,

When a hazy gleam surged outwards
From a chasm deep in Space.
And its eldritch light grew brighter,
Darting swiftly 'cross my face –

Like a stream of glowing fingers
Chasing softly through my hair
In a multicoloured spectrum
'Mid the evening's breathless air.

Then the gleam became a halo
Spinning slowly through the sky,
As the moon cast ghostly shadows,
Sinking ever down to die.

Soon a shape became apparent
In this strange, unearthly glow.
Now a humming sphere, it circled,
As its light began to grow,

In a luminous suffusion,
Till, when slowly gliding by,
I could feel its eerie presence
Probing deeply through my eyes.

And I sensed at once that, there, some
Strange intelligence looked down,
One that watched with eyes unblinking
O'er the sombre, sleeping town.

Then the phosphorescent globule
Glided silently away,
In a cosmic orb of aura
Through the heavens draped in grey,

Till its weird, fluorescent image
Faded slowly from my sight.
And my eyes were left to wander
Through the shadows of the night.

But that alien aurora
Still cast shivers o'er my face,
As I gazed in spellbound wonder
Through the catacombs of Space,

In the fear that one dark night it
Will return amid the gloom,
Like a strange, unearthly phantom
From the abysses of Doom.

Haunted houses are normally ten a penny, nothing special – but this poem's ghost-associated cottage is very special, very different, as you will discover…

The Haunted Cottage

Deep in a green woodland vale wrapped in sunbeams
Stands a small cottage, alone and afar;
Windows still shining, transparent and lucent,
Each pane alight like a shimmering star.

Over the walls clings a shroud of green ivy,
Crisp arrowed leaves shot with yellowing veins;
Emerald spear-heads outsplayed in the sunlight,
Beaming and gleaming from warm noontide rain.

Briars glisten softly with wet, fragrant roses,
Sending forth beauty in sweet-scented bliss;
Each one half-opened as if still in slumber,
Waiting for Summer's awakening kiss.

Swallows skim swiftly from chimney to gable,
Mazarine star-bolts with waistcoats of flame;
Aerial gymnasts each vaulting o'er cloudlets,
Chasing and racing in sky-diving games.

Spiders spin curtains of gossamer fabric,
Hanging serenely from windows and walls;
Light as the soft gauzy drapings of Faerie,
Murals suspended in Oberon's halls.

Blossom drifts gently down over the cottage,
Apple and cherry cast far from above;
Fragile and fragrant it sails on the zephyr,
Borne on the wingtips of Nature's warm love.

So it seems strange that this cottage is haunted –
For, if we enter its small shaded rooms,
Phantoms ne'er loom forth to frighten or mutter,
Nothing appears from the shadows and gloom.

But if we let this small cottage's image
Out of our sight for a moment or less,
When we look back, we will search for it vainly –
For it has gone, we will have to confess.

Although no spectres appear in its bedrooms,
There is a phantom of which it can boast.
And its strange secret it holds to this day – for
This lonely cottage itself is the ghost.

This wouldn't be a book of mine if cryptozoology didn't rear its head in it somewhere! So here, for mystery beast lovers everywhere, is a little snippet of crypto-history – the very first piece of writing that I ever penned (over 40 years ago!) in relation to the most famous cryptid of all. Nessie, this one's for you!

The Loch Ness Monster

Through swirling mists of early morn,
Across the loch's dull light,
A dark shape moves with hidden power,
Then disappears from sight
Beneath Loch Ness's murky cloak
Of water black and cold.
What lives in this vast underworld,
In Ness's misty fold?

What creature thrives below the waves,
Beneath the surface grim?
What beast appears in photographs –
Obscure, opaque, and dim?
What creature gave the myths and tales
From bygone days new fame?
Of water horses, fierce, malign,
Which from the waters came,
To strike the hearts of every man
With terror of their forms.
The kelpies – dark, malignant ghosts,
And harbingers of storms.

So what gave all these legends life –
A creature huge in size,
With tiny horns and rhomboid limbs,
And glowing, deathless eyes?
A relic from the ancient past,
Disturbed by modern worlds?
It will be long, indeed, before
This secret is unfurled.

Hidden deep within the shadowed lands of Faerie is the garden of their king, Oberon – a setting of magical delight, where shy unicorns roam in freedom, bright flowers sing with dulcet voices, and Oberon's entrancing queen, Mab, reposes in sunlit splendour. Let us step inside this enchanted place for a moment, and see what we shall see...

Oberon's Garden

Sing, yellow linnet, of Oberon's garden –
Mystical, wonderful, strange to behold,
Hidden away in the deep realms of Faerie,
Dappled in shadows of green and of gold.

Here singing flowers trill their soft lilting music,
Violets, red roses, and other fair blooms,
Borne from all seasons to serenade softly
Oberon, resting in gossamer rooms.

And through these gardens enchanted and lovely
Bright wingèd steeds flit from rainbows to streams.
Timid and shy, here the unicorns frolic,
Misty and distant as overnight dreams.

Pixies race swiftly on glittering beetles,
Harnessed with gossamer, saddled with leaves,
Past tinkling fountains and waterfalls tumbling,
Through groves and woodlands each chariot weaves.

Mab lies serenely in deep beds of sunshine,
Graceful and pale as the bright morning star,
Strange fairy beauty, enchanting and mystic,
Born in a land that lies hidden afar.

Now, as the evening draws o'er this strange setting,
Stars twinkle softly like lanterns of Night,
And when we look back at Oberon's garden,
We shall find that it has vanished from sight.

It has slipped back to the kingdom it came from,
Back to the fairyland realms of the past,
For in our world nothing lives on forever –
Not even fairies forever may last.

Scientists tell us that seafarers' stories of mermaids were really based upon sightings of seals, manatees, and other homely-looking marine mammals – a far cry, indeed, if true, from the bewitchingly beautiful mermaid of legend, as encountered in the following poem.

Perchance a Mermaid?

Raised through the laughter of shimmering oceans
Rests a lone pinnacle, gloomy and grey,
Sombre in form 'gainst a bright turquoise surface,
Silently cursing the coming of Day.

But, as the spirals of ripple and wavelet
Gently embellish this courtier of Night,
High on its peak – as the dawn now exposes,
Bathing her softly in fountains of light –

Slumbers a mermaid 'neath blankets of bubbles
Cast from the surface in shining array.
And as she wakens, they flit from her bedside,
Kissing her fondly like transient fays.

Slowly she rises, and smiles at the sunlight,
Dancing in sprays of bright saffron and gold.
And as she rests there, her glittering fishtail
Swirls in the depths of the sea's liquid folds,

Spinning each wave like a radiant vortex,
Twirling through chateaux of coral and shells,
Chasing a seahorse with fluted adornments
Gaily through undersea valleys and dells.

And as the ocean caresses her gently,
Zephyrs flit long through her shimmering hair,
Stroking it softly with murmuring fingers,
Kissing each rivulet, golden and fair,

Beaming like waterfalls gleaming and lucent,
Gaily cascading in glistening light,
As she combs slowly through each ruffling ringlet,
Holding a murex shell pearly and white,

Calmly reposing 'neath heavens of glory
Caught in the ocean's reflection of blue,
While, as its mirror refracts their resplendence,
Rays filter downwards in spectrum-split hues

Each to disperse through the sea's silent darkness,
Lighting its kingdom with shadows of green,
Piercing its dreaming with malachite shaftlets,
Darting with arrows of aquamarine.

And as the morn flushes brightly in Heaven,
Clouds drift so slowly by, moving e'er on.
Then, as the sun gazes down on the mermaid,
Swiftly she glides through the waves, and is gone –

Drawn through the sea as its echoing whispers
Sail on the breeze, gusting out and away,
Far to horizons where shores gently slumber,
Lit by the reincarnation of Day.

The inspiration for this poem came from Maurice Maeterlinck's classic play, The Blue Bird, *a delightful fantasy work first produced in 1908 that seems nowadays to have become almost forgotten, yet which is filled with wonderfully evocative scenes and imaginative personifications.*

The Pool of Dreams

'Midst the cerulean heavens
Lies the fabled Pool of Dreams,
Veiled in rosy mists of Slumber
Casting tender lilac beams
Through its cyanescent waters
To its darkened depths of blue,
Each transforming purple ripples
Into iridescent hues
Racing swiftly o'er its surface
Like a phalanx borne from Light,
Flitting rainbows glinting brightly
'Ere they disappear from sight.

For the dreams of sleeping mankind
Lie within this glossy pool,
Which releases them like phantoms
To emerge through evenings cool
In the drowsing worlds of mortals –
Empty shadows of the mind,
Which with rapturous enchantment
Mortals' conscious spirits bind,
Till the morning's pale suffusion
Rises softly through the sky,
Then away through twilit heavens
To the Pool of Dreams they fly.

And within its silken waters
Lies each tiny unborn child,
Sleeping long in drowsy silence,
As the Pool's reflection mild
Shines upon these infant dreamers,
Till their mothers softly pray,
Then they wake from golden slumber,
And are borne on sunlit rays
Down to Earth, where every mother
Will, her newborn babes, embrace,
As their tiny eyes then open
And behold their mother's face.

Yet among the Pool's clear waters
Lies a dead child, for he lay
So entranced within his slumber
That he dreamt his life away.
But the angels take him softly
On their snowy wings of Peace,
For from Life's harsh world beneath them
They have given him release.
Now between the clouds of violet
Like a cherub winged he flies,
To the Glory that is Heaven,
'Midst the splendour of the skies.

As a teenager at school, I was impressed enough by a scraperboard picture of a star steed produced by a friend to purchase it from him for the princely sum of £5, and also to write the following poem in homage to the celestial stallion that it portrays. Over 30 years later, that picture can be seen on this book's front cover.

The Star Horse

Into the sea's erupting foam,
Concealed by Evening's shades,
A star descends from Heaven's vale
'Ere Twilight's beauty fades.

And from the sapphire turbulence
A starry beam is borne –
A hazy mist of twinkling light,
A strange, auroral dawn.

And soon an outline bright appears
Within this gleaming force –
A silhouette in silver, of
A shining, starlit horse,

Emerging from the bubbling depths
With sparkling, ruffling mane,
And eyes that dart like icy stars
From Evening's dappled train.

His body glints with rippling light
As clear as starfire rays –
A flowing spirit borne through Space
To islands far away,

To race across the mauve lagoons
'Neath Heaven's silent gaze.
And though the moon sends clouded light,
She knows he ne'er long stays.

For soon the sky recalls this steed
Of starry, dreaming Space.
And so he leaves on sparkling hooves
Past Earth's immortal face.

From Space into Eternity
He goes where none have flown,
A spirit wild with nature mild,
A ghost fore'er alone

Amongst a vast Infinity
That stretches ever on,
A phantom flitting long till Dawn
Arrives to see him gone.

But Evening watches o'er this steed
From far-off realms sublime,
And still the fourth dimension waits
For him – the soul of Time.

No-one who has visited Stonehenge, as I first did a decade or so ago, can fail to be impressed by its aloof, stark grandeur, embodying a remote agelessness that effortlessly transcends the tedious minutiae of our modern-day world – hearkening back instead to an unimaginably distant time, yet quite conceivably lingering on, unblemished, long after we have vanished elsewhere, leaving behind a dead, desecrated planet to this ancient monument's silent, eternal vigil.

Stonehenge

Like a ring of empty windows
'Neath the mirrors of the sky,
Draped in silhouettes of Silence
As the evening's phantoms die

In the hush of newborn Morning
From the clouds each hung in sleep,
While the moon sinks down to slumber
And the stars so softly weep.

But these pinnacles of Shadow
Notice not those tears of dew,
Theirs is Past alone – not Present –
From which long ago they grew

Changing ne'er, as if forgotten
By the sentinels of Time,
While the winds breathe murmured echoes
Like a stream of ghostly chimes

Through their empty arching doorways
To the meadows of the Past,
For their pagan ring of darkness
Seems forever more to last,

Like a cold, unending nimbus
Where the sun has never shone.
And their ancient chill still lingers
As their dismal forms stretch on

In a mesmerising circle,
Like a world removed from all,
While the years flit by, pale shadows
'Neath their stony, rugged walls.

They have watched the silver starships
Glide away through silent Space,
Growing fainter every moment
Till they passed beyond their face.

And behind, a dying planet
Drew its last polluted breath
'Neath a shroud of radiation
'Ere it sank away to death.

Yet these sombre tombs of Silence
Lingered still though all had gone,
Penetrating through the darkness
As their forms stretched ever on.

They – alone – who could not crumble;
They – alone – who could not die;
Still persisting, silhouetted
'Gainst a vacant, empty sky.

What would happen, I wonder, if, tired of being slain by knights errant, the ancient dragons of evil decided to adopt new guises in order to survive and continue spreading their malign influence within the modern world of mankind?

Transforming the Dragon

Are you there, o monstrous dragon,
Coal-black scales like pools of Night?
Are your hellfire eyes still burning,
Flaming orbs of scarlet light?

Do your spiralled horns still glitter
On your brow like evil towers?
And your heart of bitter longing,
Does it bloom like fiery flowers?

Old you are, yet ever-changing,
No more gusts of toxic breath,
Spurts of fire through roaring nostrils,
Beating wings, or gaze of death.

Smitten by St George's valour,
Risen now to strike anew,
Born again in new disguises,
More deceptive now, as through

All the lands you steal unnoticed,
No more talons, scales, or flame.
Now you dress in human garments,
Yet your soul remains the same –

Tempting human minds to vanquish
All the love they know is true,
In the guise of friends or kinsfolk,
Those that they feel closest to.

So beware of all such dragons,
Different though they may have grown.
They alone Death dare not call on,
Lest they turn e'en him to stone.

The concept of Quetzalcoatl – an Aztec serpent god adorned with feathers rather than scales, and gifted with the ability to soar majestically through the heavens without needing wings – is one that has long fascinated me, so it was inevitable that sooner or later I would attempt to capture the wonder of this spectacular reptilian deity in verse.

A Tribute to Quetzalcoatl

Green feathered serpent like Heaven's liana,
Plumes of bright malachite, jasper, and jade,
Furled in bright flourishes, dazzling in glory,
Verdurous rays borne on emerald blades.

And, as you gleam in your jewel-clustered temple,
Coils gliding over your tributes of gold,
Ruby eyes glow with the flames of the cosmos,
Deadly yet passionate, blazing but cold.

Now, as your lightning-forked tongue flickers brightly,
Sibilant breath hissing softly and long,
Bowing before you in rapt veneration
Kneel your disciples in reverent throngs.

Yet, do you laugh at these weak, puny mortals,
Scuttling like ants in the fire of your gaze,
Shielding their eyes in the depths of your shadow –
Turquoise and terrible, willing their praise?

Quetzalcoatl – ophidian idol,
Soaring through Space like a radiant stream.
Aztec divinity, ageless, eternal –
Incarnate god, or a deified dream?

Over the years, I've written a number of short compositions, rhyming and non-rhyming, to serve mostly as chapter openers for a variety of different publications (and sometimes even using a pseudonym), but which, I feel, deserve the opportunity to stand alone in their own right as poetry. Here is a brief, representative selection.

The Unicorn

A shaft of bright golden sunbeams broke through the leafy canopy of the forest, illuminating a clearing deep within its verdant, secluded heart - and also illuminating a wondrous creature, standing sedately like a living statue hewn from shimmering starlight.

It resembled an elegant snowy-hued horse, but its noble brow bore a single, central horn - long and finely spiralled, upon which the sunbeams joyfully danced.

Here was the forest guardian, the very spirit of nature incarnate - for this was that most rare and fabulous of animals, the unicorn.

Suddenly, however, the distant sound of a hunting horn pierced the stillness of this magical scene.

Instantly alert, the unicorn raised its head, momentarily betraying flickers of alarm, and of sadness too, within its shining eyes.

Then, as softly as the echo of a single heartbeat, it was gone, lost to human sight and knowledge within its woodland sanctuary.

Dragons

Dragons!

Fire-belching damsel devourers mortally skewered upon a valiant knight's lance, or ethereal serpentine deities wafting languorously through the skies in celestial tranquillity.

Vermiform monsters with coils of steel, or winged wonders with jewel-encrusted scales.

Bat-winged nightmares that terrorise and desecrate with volcanic gullets of flame, or poly-chromatic dream beasts soaring heavenward upon iridescent plumes of crystalline glory.

Personifications of malevolence or beneficence, paganism or purity, death and devastation, life and fertility, good or evil.

All of these varied, contradictory concepts are embodied and embedded within that single magical word!

Tattoos

Our tattoos are the stained-glass windows of our soul,
Which illuminate and animate our drab external shell
With the dreams, fantasies, and desires
Of our transient mortal existence
Within the mundane, earthbound realm of reality.

Mirabilis

Let not the dream pervade these living hours,
Lest the winged cats of nightmare stalk once more
The haunted spires of distant memory,
Their pinions raised, alert and poised
To deny the conscious dawn.

The Panther

Velveteen silhouette, silent and sinister;
Satin-furred midnight on ebony paws.
Eyes hewn from emeralds, seeking a sacrifice;
Death to deliver with ivory claws.

PART 4:
LOOKING FORWARD, LOOKING BACK

It was the British playwright Arthur Wing Pinero who wrote: "I believe the future is only the past again, entered through another gate", and all of the poems in this section were inspired by fond memories of bygone times, dreams of what may be still to come, and the subtle but complex interplay of past, present, and future that imperceptibly encompasses our world.

I remember, I remember,
The house where I was born,
The little window where the sun
Came peeping in at morn;
He never came a wink too soon,
Nor brought too long a day,
But now, I often wish the night
Had borne my breath away…

I remember, I remember,
The fir trees dark and high;
I used to think their slender tops
Were close against the sky:
It was a childish ignorance,
But now 'tis little joy
To know I'm farther off from Heav'n
Than when I was a boy.

Thomas Hood – 'I Remember, I Remember'

Come to the Land of Youth: the trees grown heavy there
Drop on the purple wave the starry fruit they bear.
Drink: the immortal waters quench the spirit's longing.
Art thou not now, bright one, all sorrows past, in elation,
Made young with joy, grown brother-hearted with the vast,
Whither thy spirit wending flits the dim stars past
Unto the Light of Lights in burning adoration.

George William Russell – 'A Call of the Sidhe'

Strange as it may sound, this is one poem that quite literally wrote itself. There was no planning, no previous thought involved – I simply sat down one day with a blank sheet of paper and pen, the words came unbidden into my head, and I wrote them down, acting as little more than a thoroughfare along which the verses coursed, fully-formed, from my mind and onto the paper. If only all poetry were as easy to write!

Borne Into Tomorrow

The webs of Night draw back their gowns
As rosy clouds of Morning
Pass softly through the waking sky,
While still the sun lies yawning
Beneath a drape of starry sleep
From which the dreams of Evening peep.

But mine are dreams from far beyond,
Sent ever by the future,
Like golden keys to shrouded doors
Of Nature's hidden sutures.
For these, my life must make its ways
Through shadow worlds and lightless days.

Alone I stand – my world has gone –
The past was mine, not present.
Now shades of Death lie all around.
As I – a humble peasant –
Move slowly through and ever on,
Until my dreams at last are done.

These worlds are strange, unknown to me,
For these I have no feeling.
And only stars may see my grief
From Heaven's spangled ceiling,
As on I pass through sombre dawns
While e'er for Light my spirit mourns.

But I must bear my silent doom
In alien surroundings,
And suffer as the world demands
Of me – a lonely foundling,
With dreams for which my spirit lives,
For which my life I freely give.

And so, though oft my chosen way
Is dismal and despairing,
I must prevail through dark terrains
Within this world uncaring,
Through deathly vales where shadows loom,
Before my dreams can light their gloom.

Yet this is but a twilit zone
Of deep, forbidding sorrow,
Which all must e'er endure if they
Are borne into Tomorrow,
Until their dreams are each fulfilled,
As Destiny and Fate have willed.

But when at last my pathways end,
When dreams are dreams no longer,
My world will call, with songs of Peace,
My spirit – free and stronger.
And I shall go, and this will seem
To be at most a bitter dream.

Some of the happiest days of my childhood were spent strolling through the fields and forests near my home. Today, many of those beautiful retreats are gone, paved over and lost beneath the ever-encroaching shadow of urban settlement, but I see them still in my mind's eye, and there is no doubt that part of my essence lingers on in those green and pleasant lands of my youth.

A Call From My Past

Back to the countryside's
Still morning air,
Where grass softly sways, for
My heart remains there.

Small singing birds perching
On leaf-covered trees,
The sun shining down on
Small yellow-striped bees

That gather sweet nectar
From every wild flower.
Magnificent Nature,
For this is her hour.

The field-mice in cornfields,
The swans on the lakes –
All Nature's perfections,
Not man-made mistakes.

And as I gaze fondly
On all that I see,
A child's voice sounds softly,
It's calling to me –

The voice of my childhood,
The laugh of a child
Who listened, and followed,
The call of the wild.

The poignant image of the clown who secretly weeps beneath his painted-on smile, whose staged laughter conceals his real tears, is both powerful and prolific, having appeared in countless forms, but assuredly attaining its zenith in the Leoncavallo opera 'Pagliacci'. It was after watching a performance of this, and hearing its most famous, sorrowful aria, 'Vesti La Giubba' ('On With The Motley'), that I penned my own variation upon this tragic, universal theme.

The Clown

Here, 'midst the tinsel and stars of the circus,
Stand I, before yet another vile crowd,
Gaping and gazing in leering distortion
Long, as their laughter rings raucously loud.

But know they not of the face that lies weeping
'Neath coats of greasepaint, of white and of red.
Know they the sadness I keep trapped within me?
Know they the clear pearly tears that I've shed

Through endless buckets of cold chilling water,
Thrown at my face for the crowds' grisly glee?
Tears that run rivers down pale whitewash features,
As all the hate and the envy I see

Circles, encompassing people and kingdoms,
All glaring at me through cold eyes of stone,
Stone as the hearts of the crowd now before me.
Gone is true love, leaving me all alone,

Lost in a world knowing not the true laughter
That I produced in those days long since past.
Nothing remains in a world ever changing,
Not even laughter forever may last.

Yet still I stay, like the great Pagliaccio,
Always I've known that the show must go on.
Put on the greasepaint and bow to the cheering,
Though all the spirit of laughter has gone.

For tonight gave I my greatest performance,
Giving my all for the bellows and jeers.
Yet did they know my lugubrious laughter
Served but to cover my visage of tears?

The ending of childhood and the onward journey through the teenage years toward maturity is never an easy passage. It is a time filled and fraught with doubt, confusion, and decisions about which pathways, in which directions, to take.

Dismissing Childhood

Alone I stand, alone with Fate.
My shadow lies ahead, to wait
For me to come, perhaps too late.

My Past flits by, my Future grows;
I ask myself: "Which way to go?"
And answer still: "I do not know."

Alone I stay, and softly sigh
To watch my childhood flutter by,
Then turn away, and wonder why.

My changing world through dreams I saw,
As onward e'er my thoughts they bore,
But now my dreams are dreams no more.

And now alone with Fate I stand,
Soon to be taken by the hand
And led away to other lands.

Yet what my Future hides away
'Neath golden shades of unknown days
I cannot know, for who can say?

I only know that this must be,
Its light is not for me to see,
For this will be my Destiny.

I owe not only my lifelong love of poetry but also my own inspiration to write poetry to this poem, which was a joint effort between myself and my mother. It began life as a school assignment at a time when I had yet to make any serious attempt at writing poetry. My mother wrote the outline of it, which I then expanded, and in so doing realised how much I was enjoying creating an original poem. And the rest, as they say, is history. The narrator of the poem is me, as a youngster; Mary-Rose is my mother, Mary Shuker; and the airman represents my mother's first husband, a young RAF pilot called Harold Hooper, who died shortly after World War II ended, as a direct result of the war.

A Ghost From The Past

My friend and companion is dear Mary-Rose,
A great nature lover as everyone knows.
She travels with me over long country miles,
Through deep greening woodlands and over the stiles.

She took me one day to her favourite place,
The sun shining brightly, the wind in her face.
She suddenly looked sad, a lone tear on her nose,
And winds whispered softly of dear Mary-Rose.

She said: "My young husband, a long time ago,
Would always come here when his spirits were low.
He'll never again come to this lovely spot,
Will never again feel the sun, oh so hot."

And then she just smiled, and said: "Come on, young man,"
And into the dingle she laughed as she ran.
We're going to watch birds, and excitement soon grows;
And a young airman whispers: "Goodbye, Mary-Rose".

My very first dog was Patch, a rough-haired Jack Russell terrier, whom I loved dearly. As he grew older (he lived for twelve and half years – a good age for his breed), he became ever more relaxed, but in his younger days he took great joy in waging war with the world outside, just like all puppies everywhere. Yet with us he was a gentle, intelligent little soul, filled with love and wisdom far beyond his species.

Patch – A Four-Legged Friend

A little whiskered face enquires
If he may join me by the fire,
For oft we sit, just he and I,
And watch the red flames flicker by.

And though the night be dark and cold,
He slumbers, reaching Sleep's calm fold
Of visitors to dreamy lands,
With silver shores and silent sands.

Yet when he wakes, he sits up straight,
Or if he's sleeping, and we're late,
He growls in puppy-thunder tones
For ending dreams of juicy bones.

But then he's up, and runs outside
To see if any cat dares ride
His fence with velvet paws of steel
That, five curved silver claws, conceal.

And if there is a bird in flight
His anger makes a dreadful sight,
As gates are mauled in raging storms
Of fury from this tiny form.

But when the world is still and calm,
Then he bodes no-one any harm.
And two dark eyes gaze up at me,
So brown and warm for all to see.

Those eyes: like liquid pools of Thought,
So dark and deep, for Nature caught
The intellect of other minds,
Of his and human thoughts combined

When she designed those shining wells
Of secrets he can never tell.
For we know not his canine speech,
As we have no-one who can teach

Us his strange tongue of howls and barks,
So we are e'er left in the dark
As to his knowledge of our world,
And truths that ne'er will be unfurled.

And yet he understands our speech,
Though he had no-one who could teach
Him, so as Life just flits us by,
Who is the dumb one – he, or I?

How many of us look back at our childhood days with fond memories and not a little sadness, recalling the summers that seemed much brighter and sunnier than they are nowadays, the flowers that blossomed more profusely, and the skies that were infused with a vivid intensity of robin's-egg blue that we can scarcely even imagine today? How many of us would willingly give up all that we have achieved in adulthood to return to the blissful happiness and security of childhood and the loving arms of our family? I would, without a moment's hesitation.

Reflections of Summers Past

'Midst golden mists and shadows cast
By summer sunbeams glowing,
'Cross straits of deep blue heavens past
The oceans gently flowing,
Glides soft enchanting sun-drenched bliss –
The warmth of Summer's loving kiss.

For here a world of sunshine lies,
Where fragrant flowers are blooming;
While silhouettes of soft mauve skies
Through mirrored pools are looming,
Reborn from silent breaths of Spring,
As delicate as fairy wings.

And here I sit in languid haze,
Caressed by wafting breezes,
Or lie in cool, refreshing laze
As sunlight gently teases,
And dream in realms of mellow green
Of amber fields, and woods serene.

And drift through lands of summers past –
Unclouded worlds of wonder –
When childhood seemed fore'er to last,
And fears I tossed asunder
As I through Nature's realms would choose
My outer shell to shed and lose.

And then, unheeded, passed I long
The hours in lone seclusion,
In worlds that more to me belong
Than modern-day illusions –
The work of Man's despairing toils,
Ensnared by Greed's unending coils.

For oft I yearn to set my gaze
Beyond the heavens' ending,
And live again those bygone days
In which my mind is wending.
One day, perhaps, my soul will fly,
And find my world beyond the sky.

I have always loved the words of William Barnes's lyrical poem 'Linden Lea', as set to music by Ralph Vaughan Williams. Listening to its evocative strains one day, and utilising the same verse form and metrical pattern per line, I composed the following poem, drawing upon the happy memories of many childhood walks of mine through the woodlands just a Sunday afternoon's drive away from home.

Remembering the Woodlands

Deep in the woodlands, sunlight filters
Through the golden leaves and flowers.
And boughs curve softly, crowned with blossom,
O'er green ferns and shadowed bowers.
Small warblers lilt in dulcet song,
As celandines in bouquets throng,
Through dappled glades and sunlit pathways,
Past blue streams and fountains clear.

Sun-shadows mottle gnarled trees arching
O'er the leafy ground of gold.
And tiny daisies wake up slowly
As their petals pink unfold.
Here snowy clouds float through the sky,
While turquoise swallows circle by,
As morningtime transforms to noontide.
Now the afternoon is here.

Though days like these soon fade and vanish
In the misty realms of Space,
With only fragments of their wonder
Passing o'er my silent face,
Yet still I live in those fair days,
In Summer's warm and blissful haze.
And as I sit, a dewdrop glistens –
Is it dew, or one lone tear?

The Robin in this poem was not a bird, but instead an elderly Scottish terrier owned by one of my grandmother's neighbours. Despite his advancing years, he always raced boisterously to greet me whenever I passed by his house, wagging his long tail wildly, and would then peer earnestly into my face with his dark expressive eyes. Sadly, Robin passed away many years ago, but for me he will always live on in this poem that I wrote as a celebration of his being.

Robin

A black-furred face peers out of doors,
Soon followed by four inky paws,
Which plod beneath his robust form
As two dark eyes, so soft and warm,

Gaze up into my smiling face,
And in them lies, perhaps, a trace
Of many long and happy years,
Recaptured still like newborn tears

By cloudy eyes windswept by Time.
Yet Time claims not those years sublime,
Remaining here within these eyes,
Which laugh in silence at the skies,

Then turn again to watch my face,
Like darkened pools of velvet Space.
And eye meets eye for seconds few,
And ageless wisdom passes through

For instants 'ere it fades and dies
On entering my human eyes.
But for a moment I have seen
A glimpse of worlds that lie between

My human life and canine worlds
Beneath those shaggy eyebrows curled.
For in that second Age met Youth,
And Life was Hope, and Wisdom, Truth.

I wrote this poem in fondest tribute to my dear grandmother, Gertrude Timmins, who, throughout the summer each year, would spend many happy hours most days in her garden of roses, lovingly tending their showy blooms, and where as a child I too spent many equally happy hours with her. Sadly, my Nan and her garden are both long gone now, but for me they are captured forever within the kindly mirror of Mnemosyne – Memory – and for the rest of the world within my verses here.

The Rose Garden

Each sunny Summer afternoon
Amongst her roses royal
A widow old as Time itself
Laboriously would toil.

Her roses grew like ruby crowns
'Midst thorns and rich green leaves.
So full of life, they seemed to speak,
Or so she would believe.

They lived for Beauty, Truth, and Life,
Like crimson furls of fire,
Whose rosy petals upwards soared,
E'er seeking to be higher.

Their scarlet hearts beat long and loud;
They only lived, it seemed,
To keep their beauty fresh and true,
Or so the lady dreamed.

For though the plants around them drooped,
They stayed unchanged through Time,
As if their very beauty gave
Them Life and Peace sublime.

And even when their own leaves died,
Their blooms rose up still higher –
Their love of Beauty burning more
Than any scorching fire.

They were their owner's greatest joy,
For them she journeyed on,
Through Life's strange world of constant change,
Her younger years far gone.

Till one fine morn she passed from sight,
Dismissing Life's dark lane,
And to her flowers her soul returned,
Ne'er leaving them again.

Perhaps one day her form we'll glimpse
Through Summer's sunlit hours –
A Queen amongst the whispers of
Her bowing court of flowers

Without a never-ending flurry of dreams stoking the restlessness of an ever-enquiring mind, the pursuit of scientific discovery could not occur – for as Friedrich Nietzsche once wrote: "You must have chaos in your heart to give birth to a dancing star."

The Scientists

Still on they seek,
For theirs are dreams,
Each thought, a life,
A shining beam
In a vast Infinity.

For theirs is Truth,
More real than ours,
More lasting.
Still on they seek through Fate's charade,
Ever.
Their dreams are Life
In future dawns,
As onward e'er
Their thoughts are borne.

Their souls live on,
For they have sown
Their timeless dreams,
Which they had grown
From a lone affinity.

Their hearts are Hope,
A burning flame
Of courage,
Still shining forth in unborn souls,
Ever.
To carry forth
In newborn brains
Their endless thoughts
In reborn veins.

For Fate preserves
Their silent thoughts
In other minds,
Which Nature brought
From unseen Divinity.

Enquiring minds,
For such are these,
Of wonder,
Pursuing their unending dreams,
Ever.
For they are Time,
And ne'er will die,
Till man is cast
From Heaven's eye.

It has often been said, and it is perfectly true, that each of us enters and leaves this world alone, but it is also true that many spend much of their allotted time here in solitude too, with only silence and the stars above for company.

The Silence of Solitude

Within these dappled vales of Space
My seeking mind is found,
Amid the empty pools of Time
That softly pivot round;
For silence, long and endless, here
Is e'er the only sound.

But in this plane of nothingness
My mind can find release
From human woes and human grief,
For here, all failings cease
To be, among the silence of
This citadel of peace.

And here, my weeping tears and sighs
Can drift unseen away,
For who can know my silent doom
That lingers through each day.
For me, the loneliness I hold
No words could e'er convey.

And oft I gaze unseeing through
These misty realms of Space,
And wonder at the sadness of
The thoughts that swiftly race
Across the pale illusion of
My silent, sombre face.

Yes, I know more of loneliness
Than I could ever say,
As silently I've walked alone
Along its dismal way,
Till far ahead a Light has shone
To clarify my day.

So many times I've wondered why
I should be on my own,
While others reap their harvests in
From fields they haven't sown,
Then leave me there in silence as
I gather mine alone.

But I have long since realised
That I must strive alone
If I am e'er to find the life
I seek to claim my own,
By reaping only where I know
My silent work has sown.

So, silently, mankind may frown
To hear my wistful tones,
But e'en in death my soul must flit
Through Heaven's Door alone,
To kneel before the Glory of
God's everlasting Throne.

So let them stare, for onwards still
My thoughts must stream and pour,
If I am e'er to navigate
Beyond this present shore,
And stand amidst the silence of
The Future's open door.

In 1977, the year of the Silver Jubilee of Her Majesty the Queen, I think that it was the Daily Mirror *newspaper that held a competition, open to all unpublished poets, to write a poem celebrating this momentous occasion. In response, I penned the following poem, but in the time-honoured tradition of teenage laziness, I never got around to sending it off. Finally, after a delay of only 32 years, here it is, in print at last - so if you happen to be reading it now, Your Majesty, I apologise most sincerely for not having made it available sooner.*

A Silver Jubilee Tribute to Her Majesty Queen Elizabeth II

Far 'cross the rich verdant meadows of Britain,
Church bells chime long of the great Jubilee.
Even Britannia raises her trident
Proudly before you in praise from the sea.

Trumpets announce you and fanfares precede you,
Children smile shyly as slowly you pass.
Rose petals spiral from window and rooftop
Downwards in reverence to drift through the grass.

You are our glorious monarch and sovereign,
Bearing our might like a shimmering crown –
Set with the sadness and joys of your birthright,
Sparkling like stars in the evening's rich gown.

Yours is the fate of our kingdom, and ever
Must you alone bear our sorrows and joys.
Ne'er can the world know your innermost secrets,
Yours must be majesty, splendour, and poise.

So let us praise you this Jubilee season,
Long may you reign o'er our country serene.
Long may your years of resplendence continue –
You are our Lady, our Light, and our Queen.

This is one of many poems written by me that attempt to convey in words a detailed picture, or, more specifically in this particular instance, a mood-picture – combining the subtle changes of light and sound that attend the coming of day with the birth of new thoughts and aspirations that accompany my own awakening.

Thoughts of a Dreamer

Softly the skies part their star-dappled curtains,
Drifting from sight as the shadow of Morn
Lights up their world with her heavenly candles
Held in the warm golden hands of the dawn.

And as I watch, all alone with the morning,
Thoughts dance and ripple from dream-spangled eyes,
Racing in silence like ebony islands
Gliding through twilight 'neath faraway skies.

Onward they soar through the shimmering moonlight –
Guiding them gently through sapphire seas,
Hushed by the whispering winds of the evening,
Soothed by the murmuring songs of the trees.

Far from the morning that beckons before me –
Stirring my mind with mellifluous strains –
Onwards they fly to where moons shower their teardrops
Downwards from Heaven as pearl-polished rain,

Sweeping the cosmos in gleaming crescendos,
Spiralling softly round turrets of dreams,
Sparkling through colonnades hewn out of starlight,
Shooting past filigree, fountain-borne streams,

Fading from sight as the morning now greets me,
Sweeping my dreams from awakening eyes
Far to the evening like pale ghosts of autumn,
Leaving me gazing at bright newborn skies –

Laughing through mirrors of radiant sunlight –
Lighting my life like a scintillant shore
Softly caressed by the ocean's reflections;
New worlds are calling – and dreams are no more.

My street of Yesterday, the subject of this poem, is a side street in Wednesbury, West Midlands, where my grandparents and great-aunts once lived in a small but lovely old house, and where I spent many happy days every year throughout my childhood and teenage years. Although they are all long departed now, whenever I walk down this street today – whether in reality or only in my mind – I never see it as it is, but only as it was – back in those far-off youthful days when it was home to those dear folk who loved me so much.

Yesterday's Street

Along that strangely silent street
Of Yesterday I strolled,
Where humble ragworts gaily tossed
Their joyful heads of gold
Above the gleaming wisps of grass
That peered through pavements worn,
Beneath the silken spider webs
Suspended old and torn
Between the ruddy bricks and slabs
Of broken tumbling walls -
Where oft I watched lithe centipedes
Laboriously crawl
On countless pairs of trembling legs,
As sparrows chattered long,
Or breathlessly in torrents poured
Out eager, scolding songs.

For here, a thriving neighbourhood
Survived through two World Wars,
And from its ceaseless gossiping
There never seemed a pause.
But all things end and soon are lost,
As progress marches on,
For Future has no time for Past,
Its ancient dreams far gone.
And as I watch, a pang vibrates
Within my beating heart,
That all my childhood dreams of Life
Should all too quickly part
Like curtains drifting back through Time,
Till, fading from my sight,
They pass fore'er from Memory
In dismal, clouded flight.

And as the leaves around my feet
In rustling dances whirl,
A tear runs slowly down my cheek
Like some reluctant pearl,
But as I gaze, my memories
Flood quickly back once more.
I see again a tiny house,
And watch its open door
Swing to, as phantoms from my past
Continue on their way,
All unaware of future worlds,
Of other, unborn days,
As like a rushing stream of ghosts
Each vision flashes by,
Recapturing their long-lost forms
Within my watching eye –

Like characters from fairy tales,
Now distant, far, and gone.
For like a living carousel
Our world moves ever on,
Till one fine day we'll see again
Those kingdoms of our past,
And then, like they, as phantoms we
Forever more shall last,
Amidst the world that we knew best,
For all must fade and die,
And pass at last beyond the clear
Blue shadow of the sky.
And as I turn, a last farewell
Upon my ear is cast,
For still my dreams are haunted by
The murmurs of my past.

PART 5:
THE GLORY OF GOD

Nowadays framed and hanging on the wall facing my desk in my study here at home is a poster that was once blue-tacked to the wall in my laboratory at university back in my postgraduate days. It portrays a tiny puma cub, its eyes still unopened, bravely clambering forward. And below the cub is the following quote from Psalm 55:22: "Cast your burden upon the Lord and He will sustain you". During the darkest periods of my life, I have drawn much comfort and strength from that poster, filling me with the certain hope that God will indeed always support and guide me, and reminding me that I need only to look about and listen to affirm that His presence and glory are all around me at all times.

I have no regret for the Past,
For the vanished gods.
The certainty of an Almighty Power,
Who harmonizes Nature in the equilibrium of His laws,
Is of greater benefit to my soul than all these dreams.

Madame Michelet – *Nature; Or, The Poetry of Earth and Sea*

What is the whisper of the dying year?
"Passing away," it sighs, "Passing away;"
Nothing below continues in one stay;
All earthly glories fade and disappear.
The haunts to childhood and to memory dear,
The cherished walls where once we knelt to pray,
Our very churches crumble and decay:
The tooth of Time corrodeth all things here.
But 'mid the general wreck two things endure:
No change shall touch them nor decay shall wrong;
The steadfast stars may fall; God's Word stands sure;
And whoso does God's Will, he shall prolong
His life for ever, in those mansions pure
Where men shall be as angels bright and strong.

The Rev. Richard Wilton, Rector of Londesborough, East Yorkshire –
'Passing Away; Or, Thoughts For the Last Day of the Year'

Ever since childhood I have adored the fairy tales of Hans Christian Andersen, but I have always questioned whether they were truly intended for children, as many of them seem much too complex, lyrical, and often too dark for young minds to appreciate fully. Over the years, I have adapted a number of them to yield narrative poems, including this one, which is based upon my all-time favourite Andersen story.

The Angel

Day was fading like a phantom
As the evening softly drew
Spangled veils above each village,
And the moon's pale radiance grew.
Stars lit up the sable heavens
With their softly twinkling light,
Like a host of spectral lanterns
From the valleys of the night.

But below their twilit kingdom
Flew a shining image mild –
There, an angel, bearing gently
In its lovely arms a child.
For the child had died that evening,
And the angel bore it long,
As it spoke in blissful murmurs
Like a peaceful, dulcet song:

"When a good child dies, an angel
Flits from Heaven's golden Bliss,
And embraces long this infant
With a warm and tender kiss.
Then it spreads its wings like crescents
Soaring brightly through the sky,
And with joy it takes the infant,
As through all the world they fly,
To the lands where once this youngster
Had found Happiness and Peace,
Where they gather sprigs of flowers
Whose souls then will meet release,
And will bloom with lasting beauty
In the bliss of Heaven's calm.
But the flower the child loved dearest
Will receive a voice of balm,

And will sing with all the angels
Each rejoicing psalm and chord
In a universal chorus
Praising ever more our Lord."

And the youngster listened softly
In a tranquil, peaceful dream,
As they passed through lovely gardens,
Over woodland vales and streams,
To the lands in which the infant
Spent its most delightful hours,
Where they'd stay to gather bouquets
Of the most resplendent flowers.

Here they saw a fragrant rose tree,
Now forgotten, all alone.
For its stem had once been broken
When the buds were but half-grown.
Now they drooped in wilting sadness,
Though the rose was still in bloom,
So enchanting, as it waited
For its end, its final tomb.

And the child sighed long, and murmured:
"Pray, dear Angel, take it too,
So that once again, in Heaven,
It may live and bloom anew."
And the angel kissed the infant,
As it plucked the wilted rose;
And the infant's eyes half-opened,
For they wanted not to close.
Thus they gathered many flowers:
Some were beautiful and fair,
But amidst their sprigs, the lowly
Buttercup was also there.
And the happy child spoke softly:
"We have flowers now," he said.
And the lovely wingèd angel
Smiled, and nodded then his head.

Yet they flew not up to Heaven,
Still remaining in the town,
Which lay sleeping in the shadows
Of the evening's dusky gown.
For they hovered long in silence
O'er a dark and narrow street
Where a rubbish pile lay, trampled
By the shoes of many feet.
And the angel pointed downwards
To a dim, deserted spot
Where a large white flower lay shrivelled
By a broken plaster pot.
For the flower had been discarded,
Thrown away and left to die.
But the angel said: "This also
We shall take, and as we fly
Up to Heaven I shall tell you
Then the story of this flower".
So they onwards flew, as Morning
Lit the dawn's first rosy hour

"There, below," the angel murmured,
"Lived a sick, bedridden boy,
In a cellar where the sunlight
Was his comfort and his joy
When on crutches he could hobble
Round his tiny, darkened room,
As the sun's caressing shaftlets
Filtered softly through its gloom.
And, when on such days he sat there,
Bony fingers thin and red
With the flow of blood within them,
"He's been out," his parents said.

"One fair spring, the neighbour's youngster
Brought a leafy beech tree bough,
Which the poor sick boy would dangle
O'er his head, and wonder how
Bright and happy he would be if
He could sit beneath the trees
In the forest every summer
'Midst the coolness of the breeze.

"Then the neighbour's son collected
Many sprigs of springtime flowers
From the woodlands' verdant arbours
And the valleys' leafy bowers.
And amongst them was a white flower
With its fragile roots preserved,
Which, when watered in a plant pot,
As a small flower garden served.
Thus it flourished, sending blossom
Forth each sunny summer's day,
And it gave him hope and comfort
In its simple humble way.
Soon it entered e'en his dreamworld,
As it bloomed for him alone.
And as e'er he watched, it seemed that
Even fairer had it grown.
For its beauty was his pleasure,
And its spirit was his breath.
And towards his flower, forever,
Still the boy turned, e'en in death.

"For a year the flower had stood there,
Lone, forgotten by the world
When the boy flew up to Heaven
Where a new World lay unfurled.
And when finally his parents
Moved away to other lands,
They forgot the drooping flower, and
So it met with stony hands,
For into the street they threw it,
Like an old and broken toy.
But the happiness and comfort
That it brought to that sick boy
Is the reason we have placed it
In our nosegay with the rest."
And the child was filled with pleasure,
As with wonder was he blessed.

"Yet how knowest you of all this?"
Asked the small, enquiring child.
And the angel answered gently
With a murmur calm and mild:
"Every word I spoke is true, and
Now the answer I shall tell –
For I was myself that sick boy,
Yes, I know my dear flower well."

And the infant's eyes were opened,
Filled with Happiness and Love,
For they then, at that same moment,
Were in Heaven far Above.
And the infant, like the angel,
Now had sweeping snowy wings.
And together flew they softly
Hand in hand, in endless rings,
While, their lives renewed forever,
All their flowers bloomed full of joy.
But the happiest by far was
Still the small flower of the boy,
For it gained a voice in Heaven,
And with blessed delight it sang
With the seraphim forever
As the chimes of Heaven rang.
For the wondrous bliss of Heaven
Stretches on without an end.
And fore'er its peaceful radiance
Shall, to all, God's message send.

But of all God's great creations
Shaped by loving Hands of Power,
None could be more truly happy
Than that white once-withered flower,
Which sang ever to its Father,
For its joy was now complete,
Saved from Death and borne to Glory
From a dark and narrow street.

In this poem, I have sought to manifest in mere words the vibrant, shimmering embodiment of power and joy that is the waterfall, as it must have appeared when newly brought into being by God during the Creation.

As Bright as the Waterfall

A shimmering sparkle of diamonds, so clear,
Cascading and showering crystalline spheres,
Which glisten and glitter like teardrops of dew,
As shadows of gold from the sun filter through.

For high in the mountains is where it was born –
A bright dazzling dancer in God's primal dawn,
Which rocketed downwards in shining array
To herald the coming of God's newborn day.

A fountain erupting in eager delight,
A radiant torrent of luminous light,
Which trickles and tinkles and ricochets higher,
Like glittering arrows of star-spangled fire.

An infinite spirit forever in flight,
Recapturing spectra of transient light
To send forth their beauty reborn and unfurled
In crescents of joy from the Roof of the World.

This poem borrows, adapts, and interweaves a number of separate strands – the legend that the cruciform marking present on every donkey's back was placed there by Jesus in gratitude for being carried by one of their kind during His triumphant procession into Jerusalem on the first Palm Sunday; the idea of that particular donkey being granted immortality, so that it has secretly survived in unchanging form down through all the centuries into the present day; and its chance discovery one Christmas morning by a group of children who have no idea of its origin or significance.

The Christmas Donkey

Christmas drifts silently downwards 'ere Morning
Rises from dreams through the depths of the sky,
Softly caressing each child wrapped in slumber –
Sleeping in peace as the stars twinkle by.

And in a field stands a little brown donkey,
Gazing through Space from an icicled world,
Nuzzling the snow with his soft velvet muzzle,
Shaking its crystals from eyelashes curled.

Now, as he pauses, the dawn flushes brightly,
Blushing like rose petals strewn from Above,
Waking the children with murmurs from Morning,
Carolling joyfully anthems of Love.

Soon they chase merrily into the garden,
And as they sing of what Christmas will yield,
One of them points to the little brown donkey,
Standing alone in the snow-covered field.

Swiftly they race through the shimmering snowflakes,
Up to his paddock with eager delight,
Each to embrace him with warm, tender kisses,
Melting the snow in its spiralling flight.

And as he brays in the midst of the children,
Gaily they deck him with tinsel and flowers –
Joyfully plucked from their Christmas tree's branches –
Glistening brightly in colourful showers.

But as the heavens' first frost-killing sunlight
Glints from each bauble and gleams from each boss,
Softly a shadow falls over his shoulders,
Sombre and still in the shape of a Cross.

And as he stands there, a tear trickles slowly
Down through his lashes in sorrowful flight,
As he remembers through centuries countless,
Whom he'd once carried with love and delight.

Palms and hosannas regaled him in triumph,
There on his back sat our Saviour and Lord,
Smiling and nodding to people and children,
Standing all round in a vast, cheering hoard.

"Why did they spurn Him, betray Him, and kill Him –
Nailed to that Cross and then left there to die?"
Still the poor donkey weeps long at the memory,
Held for Eternity deep in his eyes.

And as the children, not seeing his sorrow,
Run away laughing, the donkey's warm heart
Burns with a passionate love so intense that
Not e'en the chill of the icicles' darts

E'er could refrigerate, e'er could extinguish,
Burning in silence this cold Christmas Day,
Lingering still, like the Cross's dark shadow –
Borne from a green hill so far, far away.

The symbolic association of the poppy with the remembrance of those who fought and fell during wartime is very potent, and is one that I sought to capture and honour in the following poem – my own tribute to those brave heroes who gave their lives so that we could live ours. May we never forget them, and the sacrifice that they made for all of us.

Fields of Remembrance

Far through the countryside's languorous dreaming
Strolled I one morning in summertime past,
Wondering why this enrapturing vista
Couldn't unchanging forever more last.

And as I gazed o'er its velvet-gowned valleys,
There lay a poppy field, burnished and bright;
Scarlet heads tossing on stems green and slender,
Swaying round ever to meet the sun's light.

Crimson and fiery as dancing infernos,
Eyes filled with darkness like eveningtide's shades,
Peering through petals emblazoned with ruby,
Outwards forever to sunlight displayed.

And as I stood there, their message came softly,
Brought by the zephyr on swift wings of Love;
For, as I listened, their spirits drew nearer,
Borne 'neath the cloudbanks of Heaven above.

E'en though they spoke without words, without voices,
Eyes sparkling brightly from tall fiery heads,
Theirs was a message more real, yet more distant,
Stranger than any before – for they said:

"We are the spirits of those who for Freedom
Gave up their lives in the struggle of War.
We are reborn in the world they created,
Shedding the tears and the ills that they bore."

And as I watched them, their petals drooped downwards,
Burdened with dewdrops, each tender and clear,
Capturing memories borne through all ages,
Living again in each poppy-shed tear.

Theirs was a love more intense, more consuming,
Than could be ever disrupted by War;
Peace was their dream and their only ambition,
This was their goal – this is what they died for.

And as I left, still their beauty burnt brighter,
Bright as the sun scorching upwards and higher;
Ne'er would their courage and hope be forgotten,
Cherished fore'er in the poppies' bright fire,

Burning fore'er in the hearts of all mankind
Living in peace after violence and War.
Freedom has come to this fair English country:
This was their dream – this is what they fought for.

As with 'The Angel', also contained within this section of the present book, the following poem was inspired by a beautifully-written short story (entitled 'The Bell') penned long ago by Hans Christian Andersen – one of my poetry's most influential muses.

Heaven's Bell

Morning rose slowly through pale, dreaming cloudlets,
Peering down softly from clear, violet skies,
Watching the countryside waking from slumber,
Sending forth sunlight from warm golden eyes.

And as the song of the warbling dawn chorus
Drifted in ripples of carolling darts,
Church bells pealed gaily their glorious chansons,
Born from the joy of their bright, silver hearts.

Yet, 'midst the chimes of their vibrant crescendo,
Echoed the sound of a more distant bell,
Deep and majestic in strange, holy splendour,
Singing unseen through each woodland and dell.

Rich was its tone, like a solemn concerto
Borne from a World of Perfection and Truth,
Calling me onwards through dingle and forest,
Haunting the wandering soul of my youth.

Snow-white anemones listened in silence,
Bowing down low as its heavenly chimes
Rang out before me in infinite glory,
Growing more fair with the passage of Time.

And as I walked through viridian woodlands,
Lilac convolvuli trumpeted long,
While from the arbours the bell's regal chorus
Softly resounded through hyacinth throngs.

Still I continued, past silver-lit lakesides,
And as the swans drifted softly from sight,
Leaving their shadows on deep turquoise waters,
Far up ahead shone a shimmering light.

And as I passed through the lavender mountains,
Seeking the bell that had called from afar,
Fountains danced brightly from woodland to valley,
Spraying the vales with a bright shower of stars.

Meadows lay glistening on in the distance,
Dappled with poppies in slumbering bliss,
Peacefully dreaming in rapturous beauty,
Wrapped in enchantment by Summer's soft kiss.

And as I climbed to the grey, cloudy summit,
Sunset spread softly through brilliant skies,
Filling the world with its rosy suffusion,
Scorching with colour my wondering eyes.

And as the sun sank down softly through Heaven,
There, 'neath the sky, lay the glittering sea,
Snaring the sun's silhouetted reflection –
Here, if at all, would the bell surely be.

Lo! What magnificence! Lo! What resplendence!
There stood the sun like an altar of gold,
Raised o'er the sea as a shimmering halo,
Kissed by the ocean's voluptuous folds.

Here was the wondrous Cathedral of Nature –
Pillars of willow, and Heaven its dome,
Singing of Beauty, of Love in the Highest,
Borne from the chorus of wavelet and foam.

Stars twinkled brightly like crystalline lanterns,
Lighting up softly the pathways of Night,
Casting their shadows like glittering diamonds
Down to the woodlands in crescents of light.

And, as I stood 'neath the Archway of Heaven,
Nature and Poetry singing as one,
Still the invisible Bell rang above me,
Calling me ever more, upwards and on,

Singing of God, of His Power and His Promise,
Sending His Love in melodious chords,
Borne by the souls of the Blessèd forever –
Praise in excelsis, for theirs is the Lord!

I remember my mother recounting to me as a small child the biblical story of how, after the Great Deluge had ceased, God set in the sky the first rainbow, to signify His promise that never again would He flood the world. In this poem about a typical rainy day, I have sought to convey and contrast the rain's frenetic haste with the serene and holy glory of the rainbow that follows sedately in its wake.

Here Comes Another Rainy Day

Hear the noisy splashing of the rain upon the ground,
Gushing and emitting great cacophonies of sound.
Racing down the windows at a giddy, speeding pace,
Fluid sprinters chasing in an everlasting race.

Grey clouds hang in clusters o'er a dark, deserted town,
Streets lie bare and empty as the rain keeps pouring down,
People sitting snugly in their homes, close by the fire,
Watching scarlet flames that dart up through the air and higher.

Still the rain beats downwards, flooding roads and drowning streets,
Swooping down the avenues on liquid wingtips fleet.
Torrents team in gay delight from windowsill and spout,
All so full of movement that their very souls fly out.

Trees are hung in raindrops, dripping down their diamonds bright,
Gleaming, clear, and shining, and reflecting coloured light,
Toppling from the branches, rushing down, and then they're gone,
Soon replaced by others to repeat what they have done.

Small flowers spring up more enchanting, fresher than before,
Filled with new life, filled with beauty, up and up they soar,
Bursting with new energy, renewed by wind and rain,
Now to grow more lovely, bringing happiness again.

Soon the storm is over, and the clouds roll back in awe –
Here's the rainbow, promising that rain will come no more.
Veiling all the darkness with its dazzling, sparkling arc,
Light has come, reborn again from out of storm and dark,

Shining like an archway leading to a Second World –
One that, to our mortal eyes, has never been unfurled.
Darts of light shoot forth in streaming, multicoloured flight –
To a world of Darkness, God has brought the gift of Light.

How strange it is that whereas the seconds of our lives pass quite slowly, the minutes seem to go by faster, and the hours faster still, as our lives race ever onward to their conclusion. And yet as they depart, others commence – the one certainty in a world of uncertainly is that Life, in an innumerable multitude of forms, is ever-present.

Life – The Infinity of the World

The throbbing fingers of a clock
Tick slowly by, ne'er ceasing,
Just as Time moves on forever,
Never stopping, never easing,
In its swift, eternal race
Through the vales of Outer Space.

Seconds trickle by like raindrops
In my life, so little being,
Followed closely by the minutes
As they chase, forever fleeing,
Through the heavens still and grey
In the silhouette of Day –

Like a windmill turning softly
Through a timeless, depthless pool,
As its orbit circles ever
Round its lone, immortal spool,
Till it sinks away to die
In the caverns of the sky.

Thus my life flits swiftly onwards
As the hours soon drop away
Like a host of cloudy phantoms,
Growing fainter every day,
Till at last their forms are gone,
And the Future marches on –

Like a journey hoping ever
For a journey of its own,
As its unknown dreams await me,
Each I meet but once, alone.
Then it's gone, it cannot wait,
Nor can any ghost of Fate,

Till, to God, my soul turns humbly
On my final mortal day.
Metamorphosis is over,
And my spirit flies away,
To a Land of lasting Peace,
Where e'en Time shall find release.

Here the mole symbolises dark introspection, shunning the light and God, whereas the fieldmouse symbolises bright outward wonder, seeking the light and God.

The Mole and the Fieldmouse

Morning tossed her starlit bonnet
Far across the glinting waters,
Calling softly through the heavens
To the hours, her shining daughters,
Bidding all a fond awakening
From the shades of Evening's gloaming,
Flitting past on rainbow wingtips
Far away to oceans foaming,

Passing by a tiny fieldmouse
Gazing through the dreaming havens,
Watching Sleep drift back through shadows
Open-winged like silent ravens.
Still he watched, and softly wondered
What beyond his own existence
Held the world in sparkling fingers,
Staring far into the distance.

Yet beneath his earthen chateaux
Groped a mole in velvet blindness –
His was Darkness, Night eternal,
Void of Light, of warmth, of kindness,
Caring not for worlds beyond him,
Seeking only deep beginnings,
Roots of tree and grass and mountain,
Curling downwards, twisting, spinning.

But the mouse sought Light and Wisdom,
Moving through the golden morning,
Past his fields and sun-drenched meadows
Kissed by Day, while gently yawning,
Listening long to fairy laughter
'Neath a sapphire-mirrored ceiling,
Shot with love-lit shafts from Heaven
Till his heart with joy lay reeling
Far beyond his lowly meadows,
Blessed by God in glory reigning,
As he scampered ever onward
Through a land of peace unwaning.

On he roamed, past lake and fountain,
'Neath their showers of starlit winglets –
Crystal spirits silver-shining,
Casting far their sparkling ringlets.
Birds flew past like fleeting ripples
Through their world of bright reflection;
There the mouse paused long in wonder,
Lost 'midst such divine perfection.
And as Morning bowed to Noontide,
Oceans sang from distant shingle,
Borne from half-forgotten dreaming
Where their waves e'er intermingle.

Theirs were murmurs drawn from sadness,
Empty songs from future dawnings;
Theirs were dreams from sleepy shorelines
Crossed by pale, departed mornings.
And above these lonely islets
Diamond stars hung softly winking,
Peering far through timeless windows,
Lantern-shining, dewdrop-twinkling.
Night had come, unseen, unnoticed,
Lulling all with dulcet singing,
As her train of shrouded shadows
Through the ebbing skies were winging.

Still he sat among the starlight,
'Neath the moon's pellucid crescent –
Like an archway spanning Heaven,
Hewn from Space, and iridescent
With the silence of the cosmos,
Like a lifetime silver-streaming
Through the cobwebs of the future,
Past the gloomy planets dreaming
As they spin in spiralled orbits
Far away into the distance,
Till at last they meet their other
From a parallel existence.

Then, as one, they die together
Like a shadow kissed by Dawning;
Thus they pass from Time forever,
Leaving Space to grieve in mourning.
Whispers echo out to nowhere
In a vastness never-ending,
All-consuming, all-demanding,
As its light sweeps, ever wending
Through the corridors of Wisdom
To the hearts of all who hearken.
And for those their dreams shall flourish,
And their souls shall never darken.

Thus the mouse found Inspiration
'Midst those hours of twilit rapture;
And he knew his heart could never
Hope to understand or capture
All the wealth of God's great Wisdom,
Though his soul with joy was burnished,
As it ever brimmed with passion
And with happiness was furnished.
But his heart had met with beauty
And the love that conquers sorrow.
These had filled his mind with Wisdom,
And the hope in each Tomorrow.

Then he turned away, for Nature
Softly called her tiny foundling,
And he scurried far through Evening
To his home and his surroundings.
Yet his eyes shone much more brightly,
Each a pool of moonlight beaming,
For within their liquid darkness
Still the stars of Space lay gleaming.

But the mole sought not the starlight,
Nor for him the gold of Morning;
Sun and moon held no enchantment,
Nor the rosy hues of Dawning.
In his heart was nothing joyful,
Wonderment and love were lacking;
He cared only for the earth, through
Whose dark realm his soul was tracking.

So the mole dug ever downwards,
Till with Ignorance he stumbled;
And he died amid the darkness,
And his spirit fled and crumbled.
Those who live in vales of Shadow
Never hear Light's joyful laughter,
Just as those with hearts of Darkness
Ne'er will see a new Hereafter.

It was my mother who introduced me to the evocative light-classical compositions of English composer Albert Ketèlbey (1875-1959). Many of his best-loved compositions were thematic, such as 'In a Chinese Temple Garden', 'In a Persian Market', 'In the Mystic Land of Egypt', and perhaps his most famous work of all, 'In a Monastery Garden'. It was while listening to this lovely composition one afternoon that the idea came for the following poem, which I duly wrote while the strains of Ketèlbey's music played on, inspiring and shaping it into its final form.

The Monastery Garden

Out of the nightmare of War's raging battle
Struggled two soldiers away from the field,
Walking in silence so far from their homeland,
Hoping that somewhere a vision would yield,

One that would show them why War must continue,
Why they must struggle when all else seems lost,
Why so much bloodshed should lie over Europe,
Death being Victory's ultimate cost.

And as they wandered, they heard from a clearing
Singing and psalms drifting softly all round,
As in the branches a nightingale's lilting
Filled all the vales with melodious sound.

There, up ahead, lay a monastery's garden,
Golden and peaceful in sun-dappled bliss;
Fountains danced brightly in dazzling crescendos,
Flowers stretched up longing for sunlight's warm kiss.

Here the two paused, looking into the garden;
Then to the gate they approached side by side,
Gazed for a time, and, refreshed by its beauty,
Opened it slowly and entered inside.

And in the wonder and peace of the garden,
Each sat there thinking of all that was past,
Knowing that they could reshape the world's future,
Knowing that freedom forever could last.

Blossom fell gently upon the two soldiers,
Fragrant and fragile as transient dreams,
Bringing them sleep to escape from the fighting,
Hiding War's shadow with Light's golden beams.

And in their dream stood an Angel of Mercy,
Towering over the spectres of War,
Till, when his countenance gazed on these phantoms,
Each one was shrivelled, and War was no more.

Now, when they woke, they possessed a new wisdom,
Knowing at last what their fighting must bring;
Blessed with new Hope 'midst Despair's cloak of Panic,
Hearing the churchbells for Victory ring.

And as they sat there, they talked of the battle,
Each one now conquering War's bitter Dread.
Then, as the first paused in thought for a moment,
Up stood the other in silence, and said:

"Never has so much been lost by so many,
Lost in the dream of a kingdom of Peace,
Hoping their sons will be born into Freedom,
Praying that by their own deaths War will cease.

"Never again must our world be divided,
Fighting in vain for the pleasure of War;
Next time the war will not end with our dying,
Next time our world will be lost ever more."

Then they walked slowly away from the garden,
Back to the fighting, the guns, and the war.
Yet they knew not of the Presence who watched them,
For they looked back not, and so never saw

There in the garden an Angel stood softly –
He who had sent them their vision of Peace –
Watching them go to a world draped in Sorrow,
Doomed till their fighting could bring them release.

And as they vanished, the Seraph spoke softly:
"Eden was lost to you, children of Greed;
Never again must such war come to being,
Next time from Woe you will never be freed.

"Next time your fighting will be your destruction,
Mankind will wither, and Mankind will die.
And of the world left polluted with Evil,
Only a mushroom will rise through the sky."

I have previously mentioned that René Magritte's remarkable painting 'The Voice of the Winds' inspired two very different poems of mine. Its memorable title gave rise to my own poem of that same title, included in Part 2 of this present book; but its image, that of three huge airborne spheres, captivated my mind until at last I penned the following verses.

The Music of the Spheres

Lilting music from the heavens
Sailing endlessly through Space.
Legendary, its song is ne'er heard,
Lifting high, its rhythms race,
Filled with happiness and tears –
The strange music of the spheres.

Sailing past the shining stars and
Through the convexes of Time,
Sweet and silent is its music,
Flowing on in dulcet rhyme,
Hope its bearer, Peace its wings,
Touching every living thing.

Reaching golden realms beyond us,
Never strident, never shrill,
Blending peacefully together,
Music soft, and music still –
Melodies from sacred lands
Past the rainbow's coloured bands.

On it plays, unending paeans
Of great happiness and bliss,
And our world stands still in wonder
As all Time becomes a kiss,
Symbolising Hope and Love
From our Father up Above.

Still this silent lilting music
Flows forever to our lives,
Yet we never hear its message,
For instead we always strive
To rule everything we see,
Crushing all till all must flee.

But for mankind there is hope still
Of a free and better land,
Where all lives can live together,
And will form a single hand –
Pointing up, where all will hear
The strange music of the spheres.

There are many traditional, quite often poignant religious folktales featuring animals, some of which are well known, others less so. In the following poem, I have combined two of these age-old stories - the famous legend of how the robin gained its red breast, and the less familiar legend of how the crossbill acquired its twisted beak.

The Robin and the Crossbill

A tall wooden Cross cast its pitiless shadow
Across a green hill 'neath the grey, leaden sky.
For mankind had crucified Jesus, its Saviour,
And left Him there helpless to suffer and die.

But two tiny birds came to visit Lord Jesus,
Two small humble creatures with hearts full of love.
The little brown robin and bright crimson crossbill,
Each blessed by the Light of their Father Above.

When Jesus looked down and beheld the small robin,
He smiled at him softly, and down from His breast
His blood trickled slowly like deep scarlet teardrops,
And falling below stained the robin's white chest.

The crossbill in vain used his bill to remove the
Cruel nails that impaled Jesus' hands and His feet,
But prised with such force that his bill crossed and twisted
'Ere, strength being spent, he conceded defeat.

And e'er since that day when they visited Jesus,
The bill of each crossbill is twisted and curled,
While Jesus' red blood on each robin's chest lingers,
Reminding us just how much God loves our world.

In the Kalevala epic of Finnish mythology, Tuonela is the island of the dead, encircled by a black river upon which a spectral swan swims, calling out mournfully – a scene captured beautifully by Finnish composer Jean Sibelius's haunting composition, 'The Swan of Tuonela', in which the swan is perfectly represented by the cor anglais. Listening to its plaintive melody one day, I wrote the following poem, but I chose to transform Tuonela's supernatural swan from an apparition of doom into a messenger of hope.

The Swan of Tuonela

Far away lies Tuonela –
Land of Twilight, world of Death –
Draped in mournful, shrouded shadows
Cold as Evening's chilling breath.

And encompassing this island
Flows a river black as Night,
For it carries no reflection,
Shunning every form of light.

But upon its sable waters
Drifts a swan in snowy pride,
Calling softly through the darkness
As the river's ripples ride

'Neath its outstretched wings in silence
While it sings it strange refrain,
And the zephyr bears it lightly,
So that all may hear its strain.

For the Swan of Tuonela,
At the world's far-distant end,
Sings of Light in realms of Shadow,
And fore'er its message sends

Out to all in need of Courage,
Telling all to strive anew.
For the Star of Hope in Heaven
Will forever more shine through,

And will guide us with the promise
Of our Lord's undying Love,
Till our souls return forever
To that shining Star Above.

Certain religious stories, such as St George and the Dragon, have generated very considerable interest down through the centuries and have been profusely celebrated in the arts and literature. In stark contrast, however, there are others that have attracted much less notice, yet are no less memorable. The following story is one of these hitherto-neglected Christian legends, which has stayed in my mind ever since I first read it many years ago, so I finally decided to retell it in verse.

The Transformation of Saint Eustacius

Through the emerald forests
Of golden-hued Dawn,
Rode Eustacius, a soldier
Of Rome, one fine morn,
As his hounds bayed all round him
With dark, fearful eyes,
Like a torrent of shadows
'Neath newly-born skies.

So the soldier rode onward
Through golden-leaved trees,
While the hounds' dismal howling
Still hung on the breeze
Like a dream half-forgotten
'Twixt Future and Past –
Yet still doomed by its maker
Forever to last.

Then ahead of Eustacius
A white stag appeared,
And the soldier's steed trembled,
Then, shivering, reared.
Just as if the stag's presence
Imbued it with awe,
As the hunter peered onwards
And then, the deer, saw.

All at once, the stag stiffened,
Then fled through the trees,
But Eustacius pursued it,
Through clearings and leas.
On he chased this white wonder,
Past mountains and vales,
And the morn became noontide
In forests and dales.

Later, Evening drew gently
The curtains of Night
Far across the blue heavens,
Now dappled with light
From the glistening stars set
In countless array,
Each a tiny eye peering
Through blankets of grey.

And as they witnessed softly
The hunt far below,
E'en the moon wept in sadness,
And shrouded its glow
To give cover of darkness
'Midst shadowy glades
To the hunted stag, weary
As still the hounds bayed.

But the stag was now tiring,
Its head dangled low,
As its heart heaved and pounded,
Its eyes full of woe,
Till it sank down exhausted
On carpets of dew,
As the hounds' ghastly howling
More terrible grew.

Then Eustacius perceived it,
Stretched outwards to die,
As its fragile heart throbbed 'neath
The sorrowful sky.
And the stag watched the soldier
With eyes dark and mild,
For it made no swift movement,
Yet cried like a child.

Then a pale shaft of moonlight
Fell softly from Space,
And its shimmering beauty
Lit up the deer's face.
And as all the world waited,
The stag raised its head.
Its mouth opened, and then, with
A human voice, said:

"Why dost thou still pursueth
Me long through the trees?
I am Christ," as Eustacius
Dropped low to his knees.
For the stag was surrounded
By radiant light,
Like a star incandescent
That passed from all sight

To the heavens resplendent
In Glory Divine.
Then Eustacius looked up, and
Drew slowly the Sign
Of the Cross there before him –
A new saint was born,
In the reincarnation
Of God's golden Dawn.

How many times – countless, assuredly – has the question forming the title of this poem been asked and pondered over by thinkers of every nation across the globe and through all the ages of human existence? Here are my own thoughts.

What is God?

Lone I sat upon a mountain
Captured long by silent thought.
"What is God?" I wondered softly,
As illusions round me fought

To attract my mind's attention
While I sat beneath the skies.
And the hush of peace drew slowly
O'er this cloudy world of sighs.

For the Voice of God was present –
Not the clamour of alarm,
Or the roar of wreaking earthquakes,
Just a quiet Voice of Calm.

"What is God?" I wondered, seeking
One who ne'er to me has lied.
And my Conscience answered softly –
"I am God," its voice replied.

"I am God within each mortal.
I – who speaks amid the fire.
I – the diamond in the darkness.
I – the rose upon the briar,

"Leading all who live untempted
By the guiling tones of Harm,
Or the cunning wiles of Hatred,
Or by Envy's bitter charm.

"I am He Who walks unnoticed
In sweet Virtue's world of balm,
And the isles of Hope and Freedom;
I – a quiet Voice of Calm."

And as Night with veils of Shadow
Cloaked the sunset splashed with red,
I at last knew what my God was:
"I am God," my Conscience said.

For me, 'Fantasia on Greensleeves' by Ralph Vaughan Williams conjures forth the beauty of the English countryside like no other piece of music that I've ever heard. So it was that one day, while listening yet again to its glorious, heart-stirring melody, I penned the following poem, suffused with the verdant spirit of Nature that pours from every note of that sublime musical composition.

The Wild Roses

As roses bloom in leafy briars,
Their fragrant scent drifts ever higher,
Through sunlit clouds and heavens bright
To Lands beyond all mortal sight,

Reflecting in their mellow stare
The countryside of England fair –
The seas of ruffling meadow grass
Through which the breezy day-winds pass,

The shady woodlands, deep and cool,
A shining, rippling forest pool,
The soft blue depth of western skies
Through which a summer swallow flies,

The tranquil peace of moonlit hours
As starlight dapples sleeping flowers,
And Dawn's rebirth in eastern skies
From misty clouds of dreams and sighs.

All born again in petals curled,
To all their lovely forms unfurled,
In this green English wonderland,
Too fair for us to understand.

Yet gaze we o'er our countryside,
Its splendour deep, its borders wide,
And dream of beauty pure and real,
And in our hearts we softly kneel

In awe and wonder, as we hear
God's shining Voice, so true and clear,
Foretelling days when we shall see
The glory of Eternity.

There are wonders to experience everywhere in this world that God created if we only allow Him to show us, but even these will fade into insignificance compared to those that we shall witness when Fate unfurls before us the glory of God's own World.

Wonders Untold

Snowflakes and butterflies,
Star-spangled streams,
Dewdrops and fireflies,
Pale hazy dreams,
Lanterns bright, doves of white,
Blooms mauve, red, and gold;
Beautiful hints are these
Of wonders untold.

Blue isles of mystery,
Mermaid lagoons,
Nightingale lullabies,
Arching festoons,
Fairy glades, dappling shades,
Moonstones soft and white,
Crimson-tailed falling stars
Exploding in flight.

Facets of memories
Distant and past,
None may forever more
In this world last.
But when Fate's curtains great
Silently unfold,
We shall through reborn eyes
See wonders untold.

PART 6:
YOUNGER DAYS

Childhood was a very special, magical, idyllic time for me, and it inspired this section's poems, all of which I have written specifically for a youthful – or at least a young at heart – audience.

A boat, beneath a sunny sky
Lingering onward dreamily
In an evening of July –

Children three that nestle near,
Eager eye and willing ear
Pleased a simple tale to hear –

Long has paled that sunny sky:
Echoes fade and memories die:
Autumn frosts have slain July.

Still she haunts me, phantomwise,
Alice moving under skies
Never seen by waking eyes.

Children yet, the tale to hear,
Eager eye and willing ear,
Lovingly shall nestle near.

In a Wonderland they lie,
Dreaming as the days go by,
Dreaming as the summers die:

Ever drifting down the stream –
Lingering in the golden gleam –
Life, what is it but a dream?

Lewis Carroll – *Through the Looking Glass*

In 1956, French film-maker Albert Lamorisse directed a short but enchanting film entitled 'Le Ballon Rouge' ('The Red Balloon'), which featured a small Parisian boy (played by the director's own son, Pascal) who encountered a large red balloon that seemed to have a life and will of its own. Tragically, a gang of bullies saw the boy with it, pursued them, and finally burst the balloon, only for a host of other balloons all over Paris to break free of their strings and rescue the boy by lifting him up into the sky and carrying him safely away on a breathtaking flight above the rooftops of the city. I saw this poignant but delightful film as a child, when it was shown on British television during the late 1960s, and its magic remained with me long afterwards, giving me the idea for a children's poem about a balloon, but written as if it were almost a living entity.

The Balloon

Like an animated bubble
Bobbing gaily through the sky,
Nodding happily to cloudlets
As it gently dances by.

Spinning swiftly o'er the meadows,
Just a merry, bouncing clown,
Bowing joyfully to Heaven
As it spirals up and down.

Soon it whirls amidst the woodlands,
Here a gaudy, twirling sphere
Rolling slowly down the branches
Like a bright, gigantic tear.

Then some splinters stroke it softly
As around the trees it wends,
But their fond embrace is fatal,
And its life is at an end –

Bursting loudly into pieces;
But, as hours so swiftly pass,
Who will miss a merry bubble
Lying dead amongst the grass?

Seeking to portray in words alone the light, fragile, multicoloured nature of a butterfly, and its fond association with the summer, is no easy task (and which is why I have made two separate attempts! – see also 'Papillon' later in this same section). So please forgive me for cheating so blatantly with the rhyme at the end of the following poem's final line!

The Butterfly

Butterfly, butterfly, hearken to me,
Flitting so gaily, so pretty and free,
Tell me of places to which you have been,
Tell me of wonderful sights that you've seen.

Fair little bringer of bright sunny hours,
Gliding among all the nectar-filled flowers,
Fluttering lightly on gossamer wings,
Soft as the songs that the summer wind sings.

Wings of resplendence, so thin and so frail,
Yet o'er the treetops you dance and you sail,
Wings painted red, flashing purple and blue,
Each its own masterpiece, perfect and true.

Summer suns shimmer and summer suns die;
To warmer countries migrating birds fly.
But when the sun returns, dear butterfly,
Visit my world, do not flutter me by.

These are two of my earliest poems for children, and both are written from a child's point of view. The first is a simple poem of praise to God. The second is a tribute to my brother, André, who in 1955 died when only five weeks old. He was buried on 9 December – four years later, on that very same day, I was born.

The Church

I walked into the church one day,
I felt the need to kneel and pray.
So many things were wrong for me,
The reason why I couldn't see.

I sat inside and looked around,
The church lay still, without a sound.
The altar, aisle, and pews of wood,
The building housing all that's good.

So many ways of serving Him,
Through study, work, and hating sin,
A prayer to give both help and love
To all who live, for God Above.

The Churchyard

The churchyard lies so calm and still,
The church is mounted on a hill.
And in the churchyard, bluebells wild
With daisies sway in cool winds mild.

The long grass growing all around
Soon covers all the soft grey ground,
While bird song breaks the silent air,
As people do in murmured prayer.

And many, through the years, pass through,
But some remain, my brother too.
His name – André – was all I knew,
God wanted him, and Jesus too.

Fireworks can be very beautiful, but also very dangerous – and it was in order to alert children to this potentially deadly combination that I wrote this poem.

Fireworks – Bright Flowers of the Night

Look – bright flowers of the night!
What a wonderful sight!
The rockets, the sparklers, and flares.
A shower of stars,
As if sent from Mars,
People laughing, forgetting their cares.

The bonfire burns brightly,
The chestnuts roast slightly,
The smoke rises blue in the air.
Guy Fawkes on the fire,
The flames rising higher,
And all of the family are there.

But while all this goes on:
"Please remember, my son,
That danger is lurking out there."
My mother gives warning:
"Night's followed by morning,
There are some things I cannot repair."

The purpose of this poem is to demonstrate to children that just because something is small, this does not automatically mean that it is of little importance, worthy only of being ignored or forgotten. In other words, good things very often do come in small packages – and remember, even the smallest of things has a reason for being here.

The Forget-Me-Not

Forget-me-not, for I am small,
Yet I still grow where others fall.
So blue, so true, with petals five;
Sweet hope that keeps our world alive.

Forget-me-not, for I am but
A poor wild flower, yet I was put
Upon His Earth, with man and beast
To live in peace when Spring's released.

Forget-me-not, though small I stand,
A tiny life in giant lands.
For though through taller plants I grope.
Where'er I grow, there too grows hope.

Despite its destructive nature, I've always had a soft spot for this small burrowing mammal. Consequently, I have attempted to show to children via this poem that even an animal as seemingly insignificant and rarely-seen in our world as the mole can be a creature of importance, a veritable king, in its own specialised realm.

The Mole

Velvet King of Underground,
Sending skywards earthy mounds
In the search for hidden worms,
Deep below the ground so firm.

Small is he, with tiny ears,
For below he seldom hears
Horses neigh, or church bells ring,
Thunderstorms, or songbirds sing.

Velvet King, yet blind he goes,
Tunnelling where nothing grows.
Inky black, no sound or light
Breaks this dark, eternal night.

Still he digs through soil, for Earth –
Who, to all life, once gave birth –
Pledged a world of endless holes
To its King, the velvet mole.

Time-slips are fascinating if baffling concepts, which I have utilised in this story poem. Although I haven't stated it explicitly, I'm sure you'll realise that instead of the monk being in the distant past (as the child narrating this poem assumes), in reality he is in the distant future, because the finding of the Cross after meeting the monk inspires the child to become a monk – the monk. In other words, the monk that the child meets is himself, as he will become in the future.

The Monastery

One pleasant country afternoon
Through lonely woods I strolled,
When hazy mists began to fall
In swirling cloudy folds
And blinded every beam of light,
None penetrating through,
Until at last the mists dispersed,
And rose through skies of blue.

I looked around, and then I saw
A monastery, concealed
By glades of trees and tiny flowers
That edged each greening field.
A pretty garden lay all round
The monastery, so fair
With trees in blossom, budding flowers,
Whose sweet scent filled the air.

And high above, unseen by all,
A singing nightingale,
Whose liquid trills and lilting notes
Sailed through each wooded vale.
Sing sweetly, little philomel,
Bring happiness to all –
Shy minstrel of the dusky night,
Of silent eveningfall.

And through this garden walked a monk,
A prayer book in his hand.
He heard the nightingale, and smiled
To hear the merry band
Of feathered singers in the trees,
As thrushes joined the choir,
Till warbling music filled the air
As breezes sent it higher.

And velvet bumblebees buzzed near
Each nectar-brimming flower,
While gaily-spotted ladybirds
Flew by from bloom to bower.
And as he saw each tiny life,
The monk's heart filled with joy,
As he remembered happy days
When he was once a boy –

A quiet boy who loved God's works
Of beauty, true and mild.
And so his life he gave to God,
To seek our Lord's paths mild.
But now he turned, and passed from sight
Beyond the shadowed trees,
And then another mist appeared,
Upon the evening breeze.

And when it lifted from my eyes,
The monastery had gone.
And as for garden, glades, and flowers,
Of these there now was none.
For all were ghosts from other times,
Those realms of glades and moss.
But then, beneath a grassy bower,
I spied a golden Cross –

The Cross that hung around the neck
Of that mild monk I saw.
A Sign that spanned the straits of Time
To lie on grass before
A silent child in country lanes
Whose youthful fears now thawed.
Yes, blessed are the pure in heart,
For they shall see the Lord.

The personification of Nature, as Mother Nature, seemed an excellent theme for a children's poem, so here is my impression of how she might be.

Mother Nature

Mother Nature's in her garden,
Weaving wings of butterflies,
Spinning threads of shining gossamer
From memories and sighs.

In her lap is sparkling stardust,
In her lap are sunbeams bright,
In her lap are moonlit crescents,
Radiating milky light.

In her hair are woven rainbows,
Mauve and lemon, blue and lime,
In her face is love and kindness,
In her eyes is endless Time.

She will change as she is noticed,
No-one ever sees the same.
They see only what their hearts do,
What they see no-one can name.

She lives in her favourite garden,
Maybe yours, or maybe mine.
It need not be royal or regal,
Where rare blossoms intertwine.

It could be a lowly backyard,
Only daisies growing there.
But if honest people love it,
Mother Nature will be there.

For her garden is where goodness
Lives in sympathetic minds
Filled with tenderness and kindness.
Yes, it's here where you will find

Mother Nature – in her garden,
Weaving wings of butterflies,
Spinning threads of shining gossamer,
From memories and sighs.

Representing Sleep and Nod as entities was the inspiration for writing this poem. Years later, I discovered that Walter de la Mare had also written a poem featuring Nod as a person, but, happily, he and I had pursued quite different paths in penning our respective versions.

Nod

Far through Sleep's misty world he goes,
Goes Nod, her old dream-herd.
His paths lie past all waking hours,
Or any spoken word.

With clouded eyes of other worlds
And hair like rippling snow,
He grasps his crook in silken hands,
As onward e'er he'll go.

He lives beyond the realms of men,
Beyond the light of Day.
Yet all have seen him in their sleep
'Midst Slumber's golden ray.

They climb Sleep's purple hills and meet
Her dreams like lambs of white,
And see the swan of Memory,
'Ere Dawn transforms to Light.

But when they wake, Nod disappears,
And ne'er is seen by day.
For where he goes through sunlit hours
No-one can ever say.

Yet through Sleep's misty world he'll go,
Will Nod, her old dream-herd,
Till Night is Light forever, then
Shall Peace fore'er be heard.

Here is my second attempt at capturing the delicate essence of the butterfly in verse
.

Papillon

Summertime, and English lime
And lilac butterflies fly free.
But in France, where'er I glance,
As papillons you flit past me.

Papillon, bright papillon,
So small and fragile summer long.
Gold and green, with orange sheen,
You fly through summer's gilded song.

Papillon, fair papillon,
From blooms and buds you dip and rise.
Zephyrs swift you ride, and lift
Your slender thorax to the skies.

Papillon, sweet papillon,
On painted wings you flutter by.
Though so small, you bring to all
The beauty of a butterfly.

The Polperro of this poem is not the picturesque Cornish fishing village of longstanding fame, but is instead the name of the house in which I was born and lived as a child. And its small but beautiful garden, created by my mother, is the garden described here, my own special wonderland in which I spent countless happy hours playing. This poem was written a fair few years ago, and now the garden is gone, but it will live on forever in my memory – and whenever I read these verses, which I wrote specifically for children, I am instantly transported back to that magical world of my childhood. So I hope that if any of today's children do read them, they too will share some of the wonder and joy that this humble little garden and its figures brought to me, even after the tragic event described here.

Polperro

In a dusty town of factories
Stands a house of passing fame,
With a small enchanting garden,
And Polperro is its name.

Here, along the tiny Dutch walls,
Stood stone ornaments in rows.
And in soil behind each statue
Pretty flowers would thrive and grow.

But the statues were the beauty
Of this little garden fair.
There were animals aplenty,
Laughing gnomes were also there.

There were brightly-painted toadstools,
And a sleekly proud black cat,
And a smiling cross-legged pixie
With a sharply-pointed hat.

And a chestnut fawn lay gently
With a sunlight-dappled coat,
And a gaily-coloured parrot
Perched with vivid violet throat.

And a cheeky little puppy,
By a mermaid on a rock
With a gleaming turquoise fishtail
Combing strands of golden locks.

And a chubby owl sat staring
With two dark but friendly eyes,
While a stout yet rigid penguin
Watched each butterfly flit by.

And the owner of this quaint house
Had a young and bright-eyed son
Who would play among the figures
Till the summer's warmth had gone.

For each form meant something special,
Treating each as if alive,
In a garden bound by laughter,
Where delight would always thrive.

And its magic soon attracted
Many other children too –
Gazing round the sunlit pathways,
Where small sparrows often flew.

But one night, when all was sleeping,
Vandals came, and broke each wall,
Stealing many of the figures,
Letting others simply fall

To the ground, to smash and crumble,
Then they left before the dawn.
And at last, when daylight flickered
To create another morn,

Then the owner saw the chaos –
Devastation all around,
Broken walls upon the pathways,
Shattered statues on the ground.

"What has happened to our garden?"
Asked her son with tear-filled eyes,
Far too young and far too honest
To be able to know why

Such a deed as this could happen,
Breaking childhood joys and bliss.
As he saw his owl in pieces,
All that could be said was this:

"In the world in which you're living,
There are people who repel
Everything that isn't evil –
Why this is, no-one can tell.

"But destruction is the only
Way of life that they enjoy.
This is why they broke our garden.
Now you're not a little boy,

"For you've seen the face of envy,
And destruction's savage blow,
And you'll see the like wherever
You may look or you may go.

"For this world is far too bitter,
Far too evil now, it seems,
To allow the never-ending
Of an infant's childhood dreams."

But in time the walls were mended,
And the figures were replaced,
And this garden of enchantment
Still charmed children who had raced

Here to see its sunny statues,
With a parent close behind.
For although in life there's evil,
There is hope as well, we'll find.

Now the boy is grown much older,
Yet his garden will remain,
For the joy it brought to children
Can through all time never wane.

To this boy it was a symbol
Of a true and better world
That one day, from all the darkness
And the woe, would be unfurled.

For although it once was broken,
Still it stands for all to see,
Just as Faith, and Hope, and pure Truth
Last through all Eternity.

The very young puppy in this poem was my first dog, Patch, a rough-haired Jack Russell terrier, who has also appeared, then as a slightly older dog, in a previous poem of mine in Part 4 of this book.

The Puppy

A small, bewhiskered face peers up
Whene'er I call his name,
E'er seeking to attract my gaze
To join him in a game.

A snowy ball of eager fun,
With silky floppy ears,
And deep brown eyes so full of joy
They have no cause for tears.

For like an animated stump
His tail wags fast and few,
As then he waits for my response,
Impatience showing through.

Yet still it wags, with outline blurred,
As each enormous paw
Plods clumsily across the ground
To tap the closing door.

But soon his small bewildered form
Dismisses daylight's charm,
And seeks his box with sleepy eyes
To doze in slumber's calm.

And thus he spends each afternoon,
A tiny ball of white,
Bathed long and deep in Summer's warmth,
And Heaven's golden light.

I wrote this poem in order to show children just how fragile the natural world can be, and in particular to reveal how very vulnerable it is to the destructive, uncaring actions of those humans for whom the wonders and beauty of nature mean nothing. May it be that this poem's message will linger long in the minds of its youthful readers, and as they grow older they will choose to conserve and protect our world rather than to despoil and abuse it.

The Weeping Willow Tree

Every lovely weeping willow
Sadly stands bowed o'er a pool,
Tall and arched in greening beauty,
Stroking waters blue and cool.

For the pretty weeping willow
Cries with leafy tears to see
All the sights that torment Nature,
All the things that shouldn't be.

Here – a pheasant, bright and shining,
Shot in dazzling, whirring flight.
There – a burning match, discarded,
Setting woods and trees alight.

Look – a fox, in breathless panic,
Racing through the fields and hills
Till he drops before the foxhounds,
Who now claim another kill.

See - a mother bird, returning
To her nest now finds it bare,
For her eggs have just been stolen,
By a youth who doesn't care.

E'er the willow sees this sad world,
Filled with woe, and tears, and shame,
Without mercy for the helpless,
Without pity for the lame.

And her grief wells up within her,
Till with tears she bows down low,
And transforms them into dewdrops
Falling to the pool below,

Sparking ripples on the surface,
Sinking deep in waters cool,
As the willow's greening sorrow
Is reflected in the pool.

Weeping willow, lose your sadness,
One fine day you shall not weep.
For the evils people do now,
One dark day these shall they reap.

The power and majesty of the horse has been a source of inspiration for me on many occasions when writing poetry. Consequently, I have attempted to convey these attributes in the following poem penned especially for children, hoping that my words will in at least some small way help to inspire future generations with wonder and respect for this magnificent animal.

White Star

A shining, jet-black horse I see,
A star upon his brow,
So white it glows as bright it grows,
I gaze, and wonder how
A perfect, gleaming star like this
Could be, on such a horse.
So dark is he, as ebony,
A surging equine force

Who gallops o'er the grassy plains,
Or fords the rivers wide.
He leaps and raves in raging waves
Never before defied.
His tail streams in the roaring winds,
His rippling mane flows down.
And o'er his eyes a white star lies,
Just like a silver crown.

White Star, why are you as you are,
So fair in every way?
More than a horse, more like a force
That races through each day –
The symbol of the rugged wild,
Of Nature, true and free.
Ne'er tamed or chained, unspoilt, unstained,
As it was meant to be.

PART 7:
TIME TO SAY GOODBYE…

It is never easy to say goodbye, but down through the ages the poignancy of parting has been expressed and explored in countless poems. So here are a few variations of my own on the universal theme of valediction.

When you are old and grey and full of sleep,
And nodding by the fire, take down this book,
And slowly read, and dream of the soft look
Your eyes had once, and of their shadows deep;

How many loved your moments of glad grace,
And loved your beauty with love false or true,
But one man loved the pilgrim soul in you,
And loved the sorrows of your changing face;

And bending down beside the glowing bars,
Murmur, a little sadly, how Love fled
And paced upon the mountains overhead
And hid his face amid a crowd of stars.

W.B. Yeats – 'When You Are Old'

"Goodbye," said the fox.
"And now here is my secret, a very simple secret:
It is only with the heart that one can see rightly; what is essential is invisible to the eye."

Antoine de Saint-Exupéry – *The Little Prince*

Airports so often bring families, friends, and lovers together – but sometimes they can tear them apart.

Airport

A sonic roar, staccato bellow;
A sunlit tear of primrose yellow;
A drift of summer dreaming done.

A world of clouds awaits your calling,
Through which a misty tear is falling –
A silent star of summer gone.

A silver arrow spirals nearer;
My eyes grow dark, and yours are clearer;
For I must stay, and you go on.

And now we part? A moment longer
And then would all my thoughts grow stronger,
And I would be your only one.

But now you leave like evening starlight,
Too soon to be a pale and far light –
Alight where mine has never shone.

And thus a final smile I borrow,
For I shall not see yours tomorrow;
And here, alone, my world has none.

And so goodbye, our dream is over –
A tender, fragile, four-leaved clover
That love I thought for you had won.

But now I see fate's cruel illusion –
There now for us can be no fusion;
God speed your way, the summer's gone.

Age may weaken and ultimately defeat us, the world may change beyond all waking recognition, and the very universe may crumble into nothingness, but love never dies – when all else has vanished, love goes ever on.

And Forever Shall I Wait For You

Though the trees may shrivel and the flowers all die,
Though the moon may vanish far beyond the sky,
Though the stars may shiver in a last goodbye,
I shall wait for you, though my being dies.

As the planets circle in the realms of Space,
And the fire-tipped comets in the twilight race,
I look through the heavens and I see your face,
And I wait for you, though my heart still cries.

I shall wait for you though worlds may come and go,
Though the seas have faltered and may cease to flow,
Though the birds have vanished many years ago,
Still I wait for you, on a bridge of sighs.

And when Darkness comes to fill my final day,
When my soul has wings and softly flies away,
To a Land afar, where every Night is Day,
My soul waits for you, 'cross the endless skies.

Many moons ago, I came upon the name Elvina, which entranced and captivated me, refusing to relinquish my mind from its sweet melancholic enchantment until eventually I penned the following verses, granting it a story and a reality, and in so doing releasing me at last from its haunting charm.

Elvina

When through the violet pool I look,
To see what Fate may show,
Your smiling face still haunts my thoughts
Of worlds from long ago,

When you and I stood here, amidst
Each dappled glade and grove,
And in your hair a flower shone
Through hazy mists of mauve.

And all around your slender form
The trees in silence stood,
And murmured long your elvish name,
A name so pure and good –

A name as old as Time itself,
Yet bright as sparkling streams.
And in your eyes I saw a world
I visit still in dreams –

A noble world of elvish grace,
Where you no longer are.
And only night birds see my tears
Beneath each silent star,

Like dewdrops on the ruffled grass,
Like pearls upon the flowers,
As I among the woodlands sit
Through many starlit hours,

'Ere morning calls me back once more
To mortal lands and time.
And then I leave this other world
Of memories sublime.

But still I see your smiling face
Within the lucent pool,
And so I stroke its surface bright,
And feel its ripples cool

Embrace my slender fingers 'ere
Your image fades and dies,
To leave me gazing through the blue
Reflection of the skies.

Yet though beyond me you have passed,
From my world you have gone,
With elvish charm, Elvina, still
You are my lovely one.

Endings and beginnings – opposite poles in the spectrum of Time, or different names for one and the same event?

Endings

Such futile things are endings, ne'er
Existing in our world.
For as each moment terminates,
Another is unfurled.

And so all Time turns ever on
Its axis deep in Space.
And ever do the seconds round
In spirals madly race.

For like a book when written, once
The pen is put away
The mind continues writing what
Its thoughts of it portray.

And so the book ne'er ends its tale –
Its end can never be,
As long as all the thoughts it bore
Stretch through Eternity.

And still, undaunted, Time moves on,
Fore'er through Space to wend.
For endings are beginnings, and
Beginnings never end.

Sometimes, not even death is the end...

A Last Visit

High above the greening woodlands,
In the alpine mountainlands,
Sat a tiny village church where
Dappled shadows lay in bands,

Sheltering the humble building
Where I passed one fleeting day,
Up the grassy slopes and hillside
To the clearing where it lay.

And inside, sweet hymns were floating
To the altar and the aisle,
Sung by unseen ghostly voices,
Hymn books rustled for a while,

Yellow pages, worn and battered,
Trembling in the cooling air,
And the stained-glass picture windows
Shone arched rainbows everywhere.

And when all was still and quiet
I moved out, and felt the breeze
Curling round the blooming flowers,
Bustling through the leafy trees.

All lay silent in the churchyard,
Each grave decked with blossoms bright,
And between them grew small snowdrops,
Heads bowed low with petals white.

And at one new grave two snowdrops
Stood and leaned, as if in prayer.
Both so small, but both so splendid,
As their forms shone everywhere.

Here I paused, leaned o'er, and softly
Read the name upon the stone.
Yet I felt no shock or wonder,
For I knew it was my own.

'The Last Spring' is one of Norwegian composer Edvard Grieg's 'Two Elegiac Songs', and listening to the strains of its profoundly sad but hauntingly beautiful melody inspired me to pen the following poem.

The Last Morning

Softly through Space passed the shadow of Morning,
Down through the spirals of starlight and dreams,
Gliding unseen on a shaftlet of primrose,
Dappled with dewdrops and lavender beams,

Softly descending with wings arched and streaming –
Gossamer crescents that soared through the skies,
Sparkling like rainbows as Heaven shone brightly,
Captured by Time in her beautiful eyes.

Yet there lay something that clouded their radiance,
Hiding within them as ever they shone,
And for an instant its shadow engulfed them –
Totally evil, but then it was gone.

She was the Queen of the Dawn and the heavens,
Golden as Light and as endless as Space,
Crowned with a diadem hewn out of amber,
Holding beside her a rose-clustered mace.

Onward she journeyed, through cool shady woodlands,
Lighting their gloom with her soul's golden ray,
Till e'en the trees bowed in silence before her,
Each one entreating their Empress to stay.

For they knew this was her final appearance,
This was her ultimate day upon Earth.
Never again would she come into being,
This time for her there would be no rebirth.

And as she knelt 'neath a bower of green shadows,
Snowy anemones murmured her praise,
While in the distance the clouds hung like phantoms,
Shading the skies in a grey, silent haze.

Then, far away, came a strange, surging rumble,
Choking the world with its venomous breath.
And, as she stood, Morning knew whom it called for,
Cold were its tones, for its image was Death.

Yet from her eyes, veiled by Heaven's blue curtain,
Shining like stars from her beautiful face,
Only a solitary tear trickled slowly,
Downwards to vanish, and leaving no trace.

Now, through the heavens, a spectre rose upwards –
One that her eyes e'er had hidden from view –
Billowing far like a mountain of Evil,
Shrouding the sky with its sickening hue.

And as this hideous wraith filled the heavens,
All of the planet was flooded with tears,
Wept by the mortals who lay in its shadow,
They who created this phantom of Fear.

Gone were the woodlands, each stifled by vapour
Spewed from its lungs as it hovered in Space.
E'en the anemones shrivelled and perished,
Slain by a fiend without flesh, without face.

Yet, neath its cowl – like a shimmering mushroom –
Echoed the grim, eldritch laughter of Doom.
Morning was gone, and anemone petals
Drifted down slowly to cover her tomb.

Does our journey of existence end with the ending of life, or is the ending of life nothing more than a parting from all that has been, with our journey continuing alone, in other forms and along other routes?

The Parting

Like a star in the moonlight,
Like a wave from the shoreline,
All alone with the future,
All the dreaming is done.

Like the birth of a morning,
Now the death of an evening,
For the dawning is over,
And the past has now gone.

Friends and dreams are but shadows
In Oblivion's vortex,
For the show is completed,
And the cast must move on.

Not to look back in silence,
For the past cannot answer,
And a new world is waiting,
Where my heart has not shone.

All my sorrows are ended,
All my joys are departed,
All alone I must travel,
All alone I go on.

What might it be like if we said goodbye to our life not at its end but at its beginning instead, regressing from old age to new birth and the ultimate releasing of our soul? The following, early poem of mine explores this intriguing concept.

Reborn

Borne out of Eternity, back to my home.
I'm eighty-one years old, and live all alone.
Then backwards once more, now my wife at my side,
Down through all the years from the day that I died.

At thirty-five in my young son I take pride,
A small honest boy who has never once lied.
To twenty, to four, and to toys that go 'boom!',
Then back to a foetus in my mother's womb.

The soul of a man who loved all living things –
God sends this pure unborn on fast-flying wings,
To keep up the work of a weary old man,
Who in Heaven lives for the race that he ran.

The rich, evocative Oscar-winning melody written by Francis Lai as the main theme for the movie blockbuster 'Love Story' from 1970 lingered long inside my mind until at last, in sweet supplication, I penned my own lyrics to it, yielding the following poem.

Worlds Apart

Hours flicker by,
My world still orbits through the shadowed evening sky;
The mournful clouds far past my silhouette still fly,
As I sit thinking of where now my past life lies,
Still ne'er surpassed.

You I e'er recall –
My lifelong dream, consuming being, soul, and all –
You never knew Despair, you never knew a fall
From Fate's fair favour, for you followed e'er her call
To everlast.

For your life was free,
More free, more real than mine could ever hope to be,
A life inspired by Nature's realms eternally,
So that you ceased to notice Mankind's worlds, or me –
Just shadowed casts,

Yes, I always knew,
That I was worlds apart from ever reaching you,
Your world was far beyond mine, sacred, strange, and true;
Yet still in dreams your smiling form comes flooding through –
Now is my Past.

Another word-picture, this time unrhymed, in which I have attempted to recapture via alliteration, onomatopoeia, and selected repetition the subtle beauty and sounds of the seashore experienced one evening alone with only the sands and waves for company, and the thought that perhaps there really is something more out there than merely our own mortality.

Yesterday No Longer – The Seashore By Twilight

Over the slumbering shore I stroll,
over the gently undulating seas of glistening sand,
shining silver in the pale, overlapping light of the moon and stars.

The violet sea flows gently up the silver layers of sandy shore,
coated with white surf, billowing like featherdown.

It makes no sudden, sharp movement as I walk between the grey, red, green, and
yellow pebbles strewn over the seashore,
speckled here and there with spiralled shells,
almost as if it too were sleeping,
the mauve and blue waves reflecting silver light that darts back and forth
over their sparkling crests like living shadows cast down from the moon.

As I walk on, the sea stretches alongside, endless in its volume and capacity,
rolling softly over silent shores like a blue fluid wind,
billowing and ruffling,
casting up airborne bubbles to spiral and cycle before bursting,
their souls returning downwards
to be reborn in the waters of the sea.

And as I look at the sea in this dark, silent evening,
it seems as if another world lies beyond its shimmering boundaries,
lying just behind the horizon, to which, one day, we shall all go,
across the rolling waves of the ocean –
leaving behind the silver sands, passing through the tranquil twilight,
until we reach the very end of the ocean itself,
and then at last we shall be there.

We shall have left the world behind,
our cares and our hopes and our dreams all forgotten,
leaving the slumbering sea to caress the sleepy shores forever.

PART 8:
NEW DREAMS

Since the publication of this book's first edition in 2009, I've written a number of new poems, but for the most part I have explored a very different form of expression from my earlier ones, experimenting with free verse instead of traditional rhyming verse. So I am presenting a selection of these here, together with a few rhyming poems that for reasons of space were not included in the first edition.

We are the music makers,
And we are the dreamers of dreams,
Wandering by lone sea-breakers,
And sitting by desolate streams;—
World-losers and world-forsakers,
On whom the pale moon gleams:
Yet we are the movers and shakers
Of the world for ever, it seems.

Arthur W.E. O'Shaughnessy – 'Ode'

"But Charlie,
don't forget what happened to the man
who suddenly got everything he always wanted."
"What happened?"
"He lived happily ever after."

Willy Wonka and the Chocolate Factory – closing dialogue from 1971 Paramount film

This filigree of fragments is a collection of short but succinct verses that I have penned over the years, their inspirations as diverse as they are diffuse, as elusive as they are illusive.

Unicorn in the Snow

The unicorn stepped softly through the snow,
Its sparkling horn and hide illuminated by the sunlight above,
Caressed by the moonlight before,
And dappled by the starlight all about.
And as it moved on,
So too did the brightness,
So too did the whiteness,
So too did all life.
And when it was gone,
So too was the light,
So too was the world,
And so too was I.

My Lady Absinthe

Give Grace to My Lady,
To Absinthe of Wormwood,
The dream-robed Green Fairy
Of Delight and Despair.
Delight in her smile
As her lucid inebriate,
Despair in her scorn
As her ague-ridden fool.

Blue Serpent

Gazing through unblinking incarnadine eyes
And intimately ensheathed in cerulean scales,
The blue serpent watches long, and waits longer,
For of what little concern to it is time,
When the azure sky and the glaucous sea
Are its infinite dominions to rule through all eternity?

What is Love?

What is Love,
But a meeting of minds,
A fusion of feelings,
An offering of opposites,
And a silhouetting of self?

Post-Oz

Long after the Emerald City is no more,
In a time beyond wizards, witches, and cyclones,
When Oz is a distant memory, and Dorothy but a dream,
The world will continue, the sun will still shine,
And the land will be green...

The Coming of Autumn

Autumn in auburn draws closer, ever nearer,
The last green swathes of Summer scuttle by
Like lizards before her golden shadow,
Evading for now her amber embrace,
Yet still destined to die
Within her soft mellow mists of russet and copper,
As, indeed, are we all.

The Piper

The piper plays her pale banshee notes,
Soft and shivering in silver elfin dusk,
And I am lost,
A child alone in the darkness,
With only the silent white ravens of Faerie
To greet me,
To come to me,
Or to take me back home.

Somewhere deep within the human psyche, prowling silently amid the darkest shadows of our mind, lurks the physical embodiment of primeval fear in animal guise – or, as we know it today, the wolf...

Wolf Magic

I am the wolf at your door,
A howl at your moon.

What big eyes I have,
All the better to see you with.
And what big claws I have,
All the better to seize you with.

I am the shape in your shifting,
The dream in your drifting,
The wolf in your wereing,
The teeth in your tearing.

I am the night and your hunter,
And you are the day and my waking.

Winter Wolf

White wolf of winter, of starlight and icicle,
Padding softly through the silver trees in blue frozen haze,
Its chilling breath swirling, curling, a smoke of sudden snowflakes,
Its frosted fur sparking and shimmering in pale, pellucid scintillation,
Its azure eyes imparting a glacial gleam of cool frigid fire.

It turns and gazes at me as I stand before its mesmerising presence,
Resistance is futile, is fickle, submission is solace, is all.
I never suspected that death would be so subtle, so silent.
But then the bright sun filters down from the treetops,
Down through the branches to where we both stand.

And the winter wolf vanishes -
A spectre swept past-ward,
A dream dreamed and done with,
A shadow extinguished,
A vision discounted.

The snow keeps on falling as I retrace homeward,
The winter wolf's footprints my lone steadfast guide,
I still hear its howling, its heartbeat, all round me,
I still feel its cool chilling breath on my face,
And know that one day it will come, it will find me.

And I shall be there, shall be waiting anew.

My longstanding interest in esoteric cats has already found expression in two of my non-fiction books – Mystery Cats of the World *(1989) and* Cats of Magic, Mythology, and Mystery *(2012) - but it has also inspired me to write a veritable feline fantasia of poetry, including the following examples.*

The Fire Lion

Out of the flames the fire lion steps,
Padding slowly, insouciantly,
His mane ablaze, his eyes aglow,
Amber and scarlet, crimson and gold.
A coruscating kingdom is his to rule,
To reign amid the fiery splendour,
The burnished resplendence,
Emblazoned, eternal,
Incarnate, infernal,
A feline conflagration,
Flickering in the dark,
And casting forth sparks,
As he burns through the evening
Like a candle through shadows,
Torching my dreams and my hopes
Till they shrivel in cinders
Of unfulfilled promise.
And only their embers remain,
Now that the fire lion has triumphed,
Now that the fire lion is gone.

Snow Cat

I felt the swirling flakes of winter surround and embrace me,
Enfolding me within their soft, chilling shroud of silence and death,
As icily mesmeric as the cool, purring caress of a snow cat.

Dream Leopard

A dream leopard stalked across my sleeping mind,
Its azure paws as silent as the morning dew.
For just a fleeting moment it gazed upon my still, prone form,
And then its pale moonstone eyes swept by,
Its long slender tail switched in the darkness,
And like a cool twilit phantom it was gone,
Leaving me alone once more with the night.

Moon Cat

I saw a moon cat once.
Its fur was moonlight and shadow,
As blue as the bluest blue moon.
The moon was its mistress and mystery,
And I but a moon-dream in its eye.

Blue Tiger

Once,
In a dream it might have been,
I saw a blue tiger.

As cerulean as the sky,
Ethereal yet awesome,
Eclipsing even the scarlet rays of dawn,
Its strange, unearthly hue
Filled the heavens with its wonder,
Gleamed from the gaudy plumes of jungle birds,
Glimmered in the plush, powdered wings of butterflies,
Glittered in the cool depths of a forest pool.

It lowered its proud, regal head,
Shaking it in the pool's limpid waters,
And ripples gyrated madly across the dark surface,
Skimming and shivering,
No longer calm, no longer tranquil,
A liquid mirror in startled disruption.

Refreshed, the tiger raised its head,
Majestic, aloof, magnificent,
Quelling the ripples, the mirror restored.

And the tiger's azure reflection
Took shape,
Took form,
Took substance,
Took life.

Then,
The tiger opened its eyes –

And I was awake.

According to science, genuine black lions do not exist, and I have exposed as photo-manipulated hoaxes a number of eyecatching internet images purporting to show these creatures. Yet the dark romantic majesty of such a noble, spectacular beast ceaselessly stalks my imagination, prowling with silent menace through the twilit recesses of my mind.

The Black Lion

Darker than dark,
A shadow from the shadows,
A black lion steps forth from the night,
With the night,
Into the night,
His melanistic mane a stole of sable
Enveloping his shoulders in inky might.

So regal he seems, and so powerful,
I can scarcely conceive that he is not real,
Just a figment of fable and fantasy,
An illusion of imagery and imagination,
An embellished embodiment of ebony,
A dream from the depths of the darkness,
A mirage from the midnight of my mind.

The following three poems are affectionate parodies of three of my all-time favourite poetry classics – Lewis Carroll's 'How Doth the Little Crocodile' (which was itself a parody of Isaac Watts's poem 'How Doth the Little Busy Bee'), William Blake's 'The Tiger', and Edward Lear's 'The Owl and the Pussycat'.

Moreover, the first two were inspired by a couple of delightful animal hybrids very skilfully created by Photoshop that I came upon online – one deftly combined a parrot with a crocodile, the other artfully (in every sense!) coalesced a tiger with a hound-dog.

The Parrodile

How doth the little parrodile
Improve his feathered tail,
And pour the waters of the Nile
On every pea-green scale.

How bashfully he seems to cough,
How neatly spreads his claws,
Then bites his owner's fingers off
With wide voracious jaws!

The Tiger Hound

Tiger hound-dog, hear him bark
In the forests of the dark.
What immortal hand he licks
That pats his head and throws him sticks?

Here is my darkly delicious (in every sense!) Hallowe'en twist to Edward Lear's much-loved tale of the Owl and the Pussycat!

Hallowe'en Time
With
The Owl and The Pussycat!

The Witch-owl and Wizard-cat set out that night
On a broomstick that flew through the sky.
Then drove a black hearse packed with many a curse,
And laughed as the miles soon sped by.

The cat gazed long at his feathered friend,
And purred with a smile that was wide.
"Oh big fat Owlie," he thought to himself,
How tasty you would be inside, inside, inside,
How tasty you would be inside!"

To the Owl then said Pussy: "You elegant hussy,
How sweet is your form, and how wide!
We two must be married, too long have we tarried,
I yearn for you, Owl, as my bride!"

And so, to honour their precious love,
They entered a café to dine,
And here, all evening, they ate and they drank
Its finest cuisine and sweet wine, sweet wine, sweet wine,
Its finest cuisine and sweet wine.

"Just one dish remains," said the cat with a grin,
"'Tis a rare and an elegant fowl.
Can you guess, my true love, just what I'm thinking of?
Well done - you're correct! Yes, it's Owl!!!"

Alone he now dined, the Wizard-cat,
With only a runcible spoon,
Then, wiping Owl plumes from whiskers of white,
He danced by the light of the moon, the moon, the moon,
He danced by the light of the moon.

What would it be like to confront a vampire, surely the most seductive, mesmeric evocation of evil ever conceived by the human imagination? Pray to all you hold dear and sacred that you never find out...

The Vampire

Alone with the ghosts of days long departed, stretching back in silent homage, I dream that I am gazing into the looking glass and fancy that I see there, staring back out at me, a tall grim shadow, a wraith in human form that haunts my very being, chills my innermost essence with its dread pallid countenance, mesmerising and yet also captivating me with its icy doom. I have so many questions to ask this creature of darkness and night, I scarcely know where to begin.

Why do you and your kind exist?

"We exist to remind humanity that sometimes not even death can bring release from the evil that is nurtured in life. We exist to feed upon the fear that such realisation generates, to feed and grow stronger and wait."

But why feed upon blood too?

"Blood is life, blood symbolises all that has dried up and long since disappeared from our shrivelled, exsanguinated existence. When we imbibe it, we are temporarily regenerated, rejuvenated, and reborn. For a short span of time, we are fully alive, even if only during the veiled hours of night. We may never feel the warmth of the sun, but we are sustained by the coolness of the moon and by the fire of the stars, nourishing and restoring us, empowering our living death with deathless life."

I stand before this mirrored being of nightmare, and imagine with trembling electric horror its long slender fangs pressing so softly, imperceptibly, against my exposed neck, seeking the throbbing jugular beneath before sliding within, to freeze forever my existence with a single scarlet-trickling kiss of eternity.

Why?

"Life is fleeting, death is immortal. Those who become one of us shall persist forever."

But what kind of existence will it be? Nothing but an undead, half-living, surely, surrounded by death but unable to find release.

"True enough, but that is the punishment for having lived an evil life. Only a stake or the burning caress of sunlight can end our torment, and then shall we decay and crumble, ashes to ashes, dust to dust, our long-postponed mortality finally upon us. Until then, we must linger, and hunger, and wonder..."

Only a dream, and a foolish, impossible dream at that. True, now that I am awake again I could indeed stand before the looking glass. Yet I know only too well that to do so would be futile, it would serve no purpose. How could I hope to elicit answers from my own reflection? After all, being a vampire I would have no reflection...

In colour symbolism, purple has many meanings, which vary from one culture to another. It is the colour of royalty, purification, fantasy, spiritual fulfilment, good judgement, mysticism, and even death – but above all, purple is the colour of mystery and magic, which is what I have sought to portray and convey in the following poem.

Purple Prose?

I could lose myself in subtle shades of lilac and lavender,
Immersed in a miasma of mauve and magenta,
Empurpled in veils of summer-dreamed violet.
Yes, I could lose myself so easily in lavender and lilac,
And who would ever know?

Here is a very brief verse devoted to my all-time favourite colour, and which was inspired in part by a beautiful online photograph of a forest densely carpeted in bluebells, whose glorious hue had been captured and reflected by the sunlight filtering through the trees to yield a totally bewitching, otherworldly, all-encompassing miasma of blue.

Blue

Blue forest, blue haze –
Blue mist from blue days.

From my earliest days onwards, blue has always been my favourite colour, but purple has never been far behind – its heady variety of rich, exotic, and often extraordinarily fragile shades portrayed in countless forms by the brilliant palette of Mother Nature, So in celebration of this magical colour, here is a poem inspired specifically by the panoply of purple - a word-picture whose lilac and lavender hues of blissful tranquility offer a welcome respite from the furious frenzy of hectic everyday life.

Lilac Lake Fantasia

Morning's first sky-filtered sun-rays
Trace ellipses green and gold
On a lilac lake's clear waters –
Violet-tinged in rippling folds,
Each caressing amber fishes
Darting long in rapid flight
Through its purple undulations
'Neath the heavens' soft blue light.
And the fleecy clouds drift onwards,
Each reflected in its gaze
Of translucent violescence
O'er a spool of silver haze.

Shining shots of sapphire swallows
Skim and rocket out of sight
As their sun-deflecting shadows
Stream in speeding, soaring flight.
And the sun's auroral presence
Glows from deep within the lake,
As its silhouette of saffron
Shakes in fleeting golden flakes.

Now the deep blue vales of shadow
Prom the willows bowed in grief
Dapple racing, circling ripples,
As a green uncurling leaf
Sailing round in swift gyrations
From the centre's spiralled sphere
Holds a single flashing dewdrop –
Or a willow's mournful tear?

And above each mauve reflection
Drift the souls of lakeside flowers –
Rosy, golden-wingèd cherubs -
Borne through fountains, groves, and bowers,
While the nymph of lilac waters
Moves unseen in dappled shade.
She, the naiad of the lakeside;
She, the spirit of the glade;

Gliding swiftly through the waters,
Cool and lucent as the dawn,
As this lavender enchantress
Through the countryside is borne
On the zephyr's ruffling shoulders
Through the heavens' violet shade,
As her countenance of beauty,
Past all mortals, is displayed
In the lilac lake's reflection,
Shining softly 'neath the skies,
Where the cerulean bluebird
Through the morning's shadow flies.

Not only love but life too is indeed a many-splendoured thing, but rarely for all time. So we should make the most of every moment that brings light, joy, and love into our lives, just in case one dark day the splendour is gone – for then, who can say when, or if, it will ever return?

The Road of Life

The road of life has many turnings,
And where they lead is usually hidden from view.
So we must have faith that, wherever it may be,
The sun is shining,
The grass is fresh and green,
And life still holds some purpose, some meaning, in store.

Otherwise we may just as well sink to our knees -
Alone and adrift by the wayside,
Watching our dreams shatter and perish on the stony ground,
Weeping impotent tears of sorrow, desolation,
Willing our days to darken, disintegrate, dwindle into dust -
And die.

Life is for the living, and death is for the dying. But what is there for those whose living has no life, and for whom dying is not death but release?

Weary of Life

Weary of life,
Of shrugging off the darkened drapes of melancholy,
Settling like a shroud of grief upon my shoulders,
Like a veil around my face,
Like a mask around my mind.

Weary of life,
Of shaking from my memory the dusty webs of sorrow,
Woven by the spiders in the chasms of my soul,
In the ashes of my future,
In the sunsets of my past.

Weary of life,
Of gazing at the broken, empty dream that once had lived,
That once had brought the light of love, of hope, to me,
Lost now, all over, dead and done for,
Lost now, 'midst the stillness of my tomb.

How strange and sometimes rather unsettling yet also very precious it is that a scent can suddenly recapture and restore memories of long ago that had previously seemed beyond recall.

Nostalgia

Yesterday, on a whim, I took out of their battered yet still sturdy leather case
my old trusty but seriously scuffed and very heavy pair
of Greenkat 10 x 50 binoculars,
long since replaced by a lighter, more modern pair.

But as I inhaled their characteristic scent,
a unique suffusion of leather and preservative crystals,
I was instantly transported back through time to those far-distant, happy days
of my childhood.

And just for a moment it was a warm Sunday afternoon once more,
back in the Shropshire countryside with my family –
all of whom are gone now –
looking for birds and feeling truly alive again,
alive and happy in a way that can never be replicated in adulthood.

Yes, perhaps nostalgia is indeed best only in small doses,
for in greater ones it has too much power,
and can inflict too much pain.

Three short poems recapturing reflections...

Treasure

Treasure is whatever brings pure happiness to a person.
It does not have to be of material significance or monetary value,
It needs only to lift the spirit and awaken joy in one's heart.
Treasure to one person may be dross to another,
None of this matters.
All that is essential is that it should bring light into a patch of shadow for its owner,
And make that person feel more joyful for owning it.
That is the sole function of treasure.
Anything additional detracts from its reason for existing,
And obscures its true nature.

Beauty Has No Fear

Beauty is has no fear,
Which makes it so precious,
But also so fragile.

Yearnings

Ah...
For those long-vanished days
Of childhood, innocence, and optimism,
When everything seemed possible,
And the world was an exciting place,
Full of sweet promise and wonder.

The ancient European symbol of fertility and rebirth known as the Green Man, a foliate humanoid entity sometimes bearing a pair of horns or leafy antlers sprouting forth from his brow, was my inspiration for penning the following poem.

The Green Man

Cometh the Green Man,
Stepping forth from the meadows of our ancient mind,
Shedding leaves of withered verdigris
As rebirth restores him anew,
To replenish, regenerate, reactivate, revive,
Reproduce and reassemble, recreate and resurrect.
Fertility, fecundity, his horns imbue their essence,
Erect and branching outward to embrace, enthral, encompass.

He strides from shade and shadow,
Confronting noontide sunlight
With viridescent swagger
And cuprous confrontation:

"I return, and return,
Every day I relive,
The world is mine for as long as I so choose it to be,
For as long as I nurture its nature,
For as long as I seed it, sustain it,
For as long as my beating heart revitalises its existence."

And then, he is gone –
Lost among the sunbeams and solitude
Of a bright, beautiful, golden afternoon,
Heading onward to the green twilight of tomorrow,
Where the cycle of rejuvenation, reinvigoration,
Will begin all over again.
So be it now,
And let it be so forever more.

As a child, one of my favourite stories in Rudyard Kipling's Second Jungle Book *was 'The King's Ankus', featuring an agèd white cobra guarding a priceless but long-abandoned treasure trove of untold riches concealed amid the depths of the jungle. Here is my tribute to that still-proud yet etiolated ophidian warden.*

The White Cobra

Here, 'midst the heat and the steam of the jungle,
I see you, white worm, embittered by hate.
Ruby-fire eyes glowing brightly as embers,
Deep in the darkness, they watch and they wait.

So you persist, poisoned guardian of treasures
Hidden below in your caverns of gloom,
Vaults long abandoned, avoided, forgotten.
Now your pale presence embodies their doom.

No-one dares venture to pillage or plunder,
Still are the caskets encrusted with gold,
Scattered the gemstones like stars cast from Heaven –
Gifts for the gods that no mortal shall hold.

Yet should men find you, encoiled in the silence,
Then would they see that your power long has gone –
Empty the sockets where fangs once bled venom,
Withered by age, only pride lingers on.

Older than time are you, impotent serpent,
Spanning the ages no others shall see,
White as the sun that has bleached you forever,
Ivory sentinel, ever to be

Hooded and poised, though the world has passed by you,
Dust and decay wait upon you in thrall.
Yet you live on, with that chill heart still beating.
Life holds scant terror; and death, none at all.

I once came upon a spellbinding illustration of an ethereal fantasy stag while browsing online, and its strange, melancholic beauty drew from me the following lines, which echo the solitude of my own existence.

The Stag of Heaven

Gently, calmly, in stately silence,
The hart of Heaven, the celestial stag,
Steps forward through the graveyard of my life.

Its leafy coat, grass-green amid the moonlight,
Flows like forest waves upon the lake,
And glows like living foxfire in my eyes.

Its antlers bear the promised buds of future years,
The dreams that may be mine in other days,
And I can only wait and hope and pray.

It passes from my sight, the land is dark,
No phosphorescent glimmer, the waters still and cold,
And I? Alone once more, as ever it shall be.

Seeing online a lovely illustration of a fox sheltered from persecution in a sunlit forest glade, an expression of sublime peace on its face, knowing that it was perfectly safe in this tranquil, magical place, made me think of how many ways can sanctuary be defined, and what sanctuary means to me – which in turn inspired me to write the following poem.

Sanctuary

Where might I find sanctuary,
Somewhere safe, secure, serene,
Where I could once again be loved,
Cared for,
Cherished?

Like a vale of green mists and golden shadows
Where a fox can lie and linger,
Undisturbed and unthreatened, a haven of peace.

Like a realm of leafy trees and fragrant meadows
Where tiny birds can sing in joy,
Beneath Heaven's bright, resplendent dome of glory.

Like the sanctuary of a mother's heart
Where a child can live and be loved,
Knowing that here he will always be safe, will always be home.

PART 9:
REMEMBERING MY MOTHER

On Easter Monday 2013, my dear mother, Mary Doreen Shuker, passed away, leaving me totally devastated at the loss of the most wonderful, loving person in my life. This final section of my book is my personal tribute to her.

God bless you, Little Mom – I shall always love you, miss you, and wish that you were here.

Remembrance is the only paradise out of which we cannot be driven away.

Jean Paul Friedrich Richter

The above quotation, chosen long ago by my mother, is inscribed upon the tombstone of the
first of my family's two three-person grave plots.
Here lie her parents (my Nan and Grandad), Gertrude and Ernest Timmins,
and her first husband, Harold Hooper
- who died aged only 31 as a result of serving in the armed forces
during World War II.

How very true is that quotation,
which must have been such a source of comfort to her
in the face of her great losses,
and which is now of equal comfort to me in the face of mine.

God gave us memories so that we may have roses in December.

Adapted from a line in a rectorial address given by James M. Barrie on
3 May 1922 at St Andrews University, Scotland.

The above quotation, also chosen long ago by my mother, is inscribed upon the tombstone of
my family's second three-person grave plot,
situated alongside the first one.
Here is where my little brother André (who passed away in 1955)
and my mother lie,
and where, when it is my time, I too shall lie,
reunited at last with my family and never to be parted from them again.

Beauty was hers in all its brightness
and she was determined to embrace every shape, line and color imbued in her spirit.

Quotation on the lid of the memory box that I bought for Mom on 8 April 2013;
it describes her perfectly; indeed, it could have been written specifically for her.

These are without question the most heartfelt words that I have ever written, and I deliberately penned them in an informal, conversational style, so that when I spoke them aloud, standing beside Mom's coffin during the service in church on that most sombre and lonely day, the day of her funeral, it would be as if I were talking directly to her. And so, indeed, it was. I pray with all my heart that Mom heard them in Heaven, and that they did – and do – justice to the finest lady that ever lived, to the best friend that I shall ever have, and to the most wonderful, loving mother that there could ever be.

In Memoriam
– My Eulogy to My Mother,
Mary Doreen Shuker,
Spoken by Me at Her Funeral

Hello little Mom, you'll always be my dear sweet innocent little Mom.

Well, here we are, just the two of us together today, just like you wanted – you always said that the only person you wanted here today was me, and I'm here for you, Mom, as always. We're side by side, united as one, just like we've always been. As long as we're together, that's all that matters, that's all that's ever mattered.

It would take me many lifetimes to tell you just how much I love you, little Mom, and how thankful I am to you in countless different ways, but in the time that I have here with you now, I need so much to tell you the important things that mean the very most.

Please, though, don't think badly of me, Mom, for having written all of this down rather than just saying what comes into my mind. I just couldn't take the risk of being so distressed that my mind froze, or I stuttered and stumbled, or forgot to say something essential. This is for you, so I want it to be perfect in every way, because that's what you are.

First of all, I love you Mom with all of my heart, and I know that you love me the same too, because love never dies. You've always been the perfect Mom, no-one could have ever been blessed with a kinder, better mother – you were born to be a mother, and I am truly truly blessed that you are mine and that I have been embraced throughout my life by your unfaltering, eternal love.

It's thanks to your precious love, your ever-present loyalty and support, your constant encouragement, your lifelong inspiration, and your practical wisdom that I have always sought and have always received whenever I've needed advice, help, or even just a sympathetic ear to listen to all of my problems, that I am who I am today, Mom. We were always much more than son and mother - we were also best friends, kindred spirits, who shared the same interests, liked the same things, and understood each other like no one else ever could or ever will. And that is how we will always remain. You will no longer be present beside me in the physical sense, Mom, though I shall always wish that you were and I shall miss seeing you, talking to you, and just being with you more than I can ever say, but you will be forever in my thoughts, in my memories (all of which are good ones), and in my heart, all the days of my life.

Whatever good may be in me, whatever creativity I have displayed, whatever positivity I possess, they all come directly from you, Mom. Your own love of nature and animals and also of books and literature nurtured mine too, ultimately leading me to become a zoologist and a full-time, professional, published author on cryptozoology and other wildlife subjects. And your own skills as a secretary and perfect command of the English language were willingly made available to me by you when we were checking the proofs of my books together back in the pre-computerised days of publishing.

And your fond wish to be able to travel the world one day and for me to see many of its wonders and marvels led you some years *after* retiring to go *back* to work, taking on a part-time secretarial post, in order to earn enough money to fund us on our travels while I was still just a teenager to many fantastic destinations in Europe, as well as North Africa and even a holiday in the USA. And these sights inspired me when I became a man to continue journeying to even more exotic, fascinating locations, and I always took you with me, to show you all the places that you'd dreamed of seeing but never expected to – remember Easter Island and Rio de Janeiro, Singapore and Hong Kong, Thailand, Las Vegas, Egypt, New Zealand, and Cape Town in South Africa? We visited all of these and many more, didn't we, Mom? And our adventures in those fabulous faraway places will remain some of my most treasured memories of all time.

However, we've both had *tough* things happen in our lives too, but together we've always seen them through – you and me against the world - somehow we've always managed to come through relatively unscathed together, until this last, final confrontation came along. And although we battled it together as we've always done, it was simply one too many for you, Mom, at 92, to take on and win, even with me at your side and fighting it with you and for you every step of the way as ever. On the holy day of Easter Monday, God looked down upon us and in His infinite kindness He granted you the gifts of peace and release from this mortal world of pain and grief. In so doing, He brought me more grief and sorrow than I have ever thought it possible for the world to hold, but I completely understand and accept that His decision was as ever the correct one. Neither He nor I would have wanted you to suffer, and He also blessed us with the ultimate gift that He could bestow upon us – He allowed me to be with you at the very end, little Mom, so that you were not alone, and to hold your hand, to stroke your brow, to tell you everything that I wanted and needed to tell you, and to kiss you goodbye, for now. And for all of this, I shall be eternally grateful to God, for His kindness and for the greatest blessing that He could ever have given to us. Thank you, dear Lord.

I'm wearing your wedding ring from now on, Mom, on my little finger, where it fits perfectly. So now, you'll be with me again; whenever I look at it or touch it, you'll be there, to give me strength, courage, and your support, just like you've always done. And do you remember that lovely belt buckle and belt you bought me years and years ago from Great Bridge? I always loved it so much, but I *wore* it so much, year in year out, that the buckle eventually fell apart, and I was really upset when that happened. I thought it was beyond repair, but a friend mended it for me a few days ago, so I'm wearing it today and will be wearing it all the time from now on too. And that beautiful silver-and-turquoise Nubian scarab bracelet that I bought for you on your birthday in Luxor, Egypt, and which you've always worn on your arm ever since, it's now on display on top of your beautiful lacquered television cabinet in the lounge, where I can always see it. And don't worry about the rings that you were wearing on Easter Monday, Mom, I have them all at home, safe and sound, and your big blue sheepskin jacket I bought you that you were wearing too, together with your alpaca jumper from Chile and your other clothes from that day. Everything's back home and fine, Mom, I made sure of all of that for you.

Back in 1989, I dedicated my first book, *Mystery Cats of the World*, to my family, past and present, for love and unwavering support. Two years later, I dedicated my second book, *Extraordinary Animals Worldwide*, specifically to you, Mom, with the following words: "To my mother, Mary D. Shuker, whose lifelong interest in wildlife has guided and encouraged my own since my earliest days", followed by a short quote from *Life Thoughts* by Henry Ward Beecher: "The mother's heart is the child's schoolroom". No words were ever a better description of how you inspired me than those.

I am also dedicating to you, Mom, my latest book, *Mirabilis*, the American one that I've told you about. Here is my dedication, straight from the manuscript, and which I feel sums up everything that I could ever hope to express to you:

In memory of my dear mother, Mary Doreen Shuker
(January 29 1921-April 1 2013)

Whatever good there may be in me came from you.
Thank you for blessing my life by being in it as my mother.
You were, are, and always will be quite simply
the best person I shall ever know,
and I love you with all of my heart.
God bless you, little Mom,
please wait for me,
watch over me in this lonely existence of mine now,
and come for me when my time here is over.
Au revoir, Mom, until we meet again.

And I do mean au revoir, not goodbye, so I am not saying goodbye here, Mom, only, until we meet again, as we will surely do with God's grace.

I love you, little Mom, always.

Here is the epitaph that I composed for my mother's headstone, celebrating her memory and our shared, undying love for one another.

Mom's Epitaph For Her Headstone

IN DEAREST, EVERLASTING MEMORY OF

MARY DOREEN SHUKER,

BELOVED MOTHER OF KARL PATRICK NICHOLAS SHUKER.

BORN 1921, PASSED AWAY 2013,

BUT LOVE NEVER DIES.

In the days, weeks, and months during that first traumatic year since my mother's passing, I have sought to put into words just how much she has always meant to me, how profoundly influential she has been throughout my life, and how grief-stricken I remain. Here is a selection of what I have written.

Remembering My Mother

Whatever good there may be in me came from you.
Thank you for blessing my life by being in it
as my mother.
You were, are, and always will be quite simply
the best person I shall ever know,
and I love you with all of my heart.
God bless you, little Mom,
please wait for me,
watch over me in this lonely existence of mine now,
and come for me when my time here is over.
Au revoir, Mom, until we meet again.

My tribute to Mom, posted on my Facebook wall on 1 April 2013 when announcing her passing; and it is also my Dedication to her in my book Mirabilis *(Anomalist Books: San Antonio, 2013).*

God bless you, Mom.
Thank you for everything that has ever been good in my life.
How I wish that you were still here with me, fit and well,
ready to set off with me on our next adventure together.
I love you, little Mom, always.

The words I wrote beneath the picture of the memory box that I bought for Mom, posted below my eulogy to her on my ShukerNature blog for 16 April 2013.

13 weeks ago this evening, my dear little Mom passed away -
a whole quarter-year has somehow gone by,
during which time I have found myself
locked inside a strange and very sad new life.
I can never return to the past,
except in dreams,
and the future is as ever opaque.
And so I live life now a moment at a time,
and dream...

Posted on my Facebook wall on 1 July 2013

I attended my Mom's Memorial Service tonight at church,
and I placed a candle for her on a table before me,
where its light gently flickered until the end of the service,
after which, once I had left the church,
it would be extinguished.

But the candle of love that my Mom had lit inside my heart
on the day that I was born,
and which now burns there for her,
is infinitely brighter, warmer,
and will never be extinguished.

And although the memorial service for my Mom in church is over now,
the memorial service for her that has been performing inside my mind
every moment of every day since she passed away
will never come to an end
– it will continue in perpetuity for the rest of my life.

God bless you Mom - I love you, always.

Posted on my Facebook wall on 21 July 2013 following my attendance of my Mom's Memorial Service earlier that evening.

One part of the show that really registered with me was the song
'They Live In You',
when the shaman-type mandrill Rafiki was telling the adult Simba
that his father will always be a part of him,
will always live in him,
and that when he looks into the mirror of a forest pool,
he will see his father in his own reflection,
looking back at him.
I'd never thought of that before.

Also, several people have told me that I have my Mom's eyes,
different colour but same shape and depth;
and Mom often joked that I had her squat, pudgy nose,
and I do.

So now, whenever I look into a mirror,
I'll see Mom there in my reflection,
spiritually and physically,
looking back at me,
and I'll know that she is part of me,
is with me still,
forever.

Posted on my Facebook wall on 10 August 2013 after attending a performance of Disney's 'The Lion King' stage musical at the Birmingham Hippodrome that afternoon.

This evening marks exactly 26 weeks = 6 months = half a year since my mother, Mary
Shuker, passed away,
leaving behind an aching void inside my heart
that I have papered over with memories
but which can never be filled and will never heal.
God bless you Mom,
how I miss you and wish you were here with me still.
With all my love.

Posted on my Facebook wall on 30 September 2013.

This morning, I visited the newly-completed gravestone of my mother,
Mary Doreen Shuker (1921-2013), which has taken 6 months to prepare.
Standing there in the solitude of the cemetery, it all still seemed so unreal,
that the vibrant little lady always so full of life, of living, and of love was gone,
her time in this world marked only by the stone and grave there before me,
beautiful and elegant though they were, just like she had always been.
Come the closing of December, I shall not grieve the passing of 2013,
but I shall forever grieve the passing within it of my mother,
whose light is gone from my world
until that joyous day when we will be reunited forever.

*From the introduction to my composition 'The Chained Gates', which I wrote on 22 October
2013 (and which can be read in full beginning on page 236 of this book).*

2013

I shall not mourn the passing of this year,
Nor shall I mourn its months of grief and strife.
All I shall mourn is that one person dear,
My mother, whom it stole out of my life.

God bless you, Little Mom - I love you always.
Happy New Year - may we be together again one day.

Composed by me and posted on my Facebook wall on 31 December 2013.

Happy Birthday in Heaven, Mom
- how I wish that I could share it with you.
God Bless.

Posted on my Facebook wall on my mother's birthday, 29 January 2014.

To my dear mother, Mary D. Shuker (1921-2013),
whose lifelong interest in wildlife
guided and encouraged my own from my earliest days.
Thank you for filling my world with wonder, joy, and love
for such a long and very happy time.
How I miss you, and how I wish that you were still here with me today
and always.
God bless you, little Mom.

The mother's heart is the child's schoolroom
Henry Ward Beecher – *Life Thoughts*

My Dedication to my mother in my book, The Menagerie of Marvels: A Third Compendium of Extraordinary Animals *(CFZ Press: Bideford, published in summer 2014).*

Time waits for no-one, for nothing, not even for grief.
Tomorrow will be 52 Saturdays since Mom and I set off
on what would be our last outing together,
though mercifully we had no realisation of that at the time,
and had a lovely afternoon.
On Sunday it is Mother's Day this year,
and it will also be 52 Sundays since Mom was taken ill late that evening.
Monday will be 12 months to the day since she gently slipped away
early that evening in hospital,
with me beside her, holding her hand and telling her how much I loved her.
And Tuesday will be 12 months to the date
since that most traumatic of all events in my life happened
- the event that I had always dreaded most
throughout my entire time here on earth.
So, wish me well during the next four very momentous days for me,
as they revive all of those mixed memories,
and bring to a close the worst year of my life
- a year which, if I am honest, I may not have survived had it not been
for the kind words and continuing support of so many friends
here on Facebook.
So thank you all - I am truly grateful.

Posted on my Facebook wall on 28 March 2014.

I wrote the following composition during the evening of 22 October 2013, after I'd attempted to visit the newly-completed gravestone of my mother, Mary Doreen Shuker (1921-2013), just a few hours earlier, only to discover to my dismay that the cemetery had already closed. On the following morning, however, I did successfully visit Mom's gravestone, which had taken 6 months to prepare. Standing there in the solitude of the cemetery, it all still seemed so unreal, that the vibrant little lady always so full of life, of living, and of love was gone, her time in this world marked only by the stone and grave there before me, beautiful and elegant though they were, just like she had always been. I knew that come the closing of December, I would not grieve the passing of 2013, but I will forever grieve the passing within it of my mother, whose light is gone from my world until that joyous day when we will be reunited forever.

The Chained Gates

This afternoon at around 4.10 pm I received a phone call from the memorial stone masons informing me that Mom's gravestone with her inscription was at last complete and in place upon her grave. The weather wasn't good, so I decided not to visit straight away, but then at around 4.50 pm it improved and the sun came out. So I psyched myself up to be ready, then got the car out and drove to the cemetery, only to find that it was locked. It turns out that from October to April it closes at 4.30 pm, instead of at 7.00 pm as it does for the rest of the year. I didn't know that.

Standing there, outside the cemetery with its chained gates separating me from Mom's grave, was heavily symbolic for me - it is after all a representation of the real situation that I endure every day. I stand in this life, and Mom in the next, so I am separated from her by the great divide of death, the chained gates through which I cannot pass while still alive. Seeing those gates brought it all home to me so much. Of course, I know that I have only to wait until tomorrow to be able to walk through the unchained cemetery gates and be with Mom's mortal self at her grave, whereas I have to wait for the rest of my life before I can transcend death to be with her in spiritual immortality.

Her gravestone was the last thing that I could organise for Mom, and I hope that it is elegant and beautiful, just as she always was. Mom never liked the taking of flowers to graves, as they soon fade and die, or are stolen by others, so I've instructed that a pair of multicoloured bouquets be engraved onto her gravestone, so that she will always have flowers that will never fade, never die, and never be stolen.

Visting her completed grave for the first time will in a sense mark the final footstep in my own personal Via Dolorosa, the sorrowful path that I have trodden for the past 29 weeks since she passed away while everything associated with her funeral and burial was being organised by me for her and was then being carried out, stage by stage. My grief will not be abated by my visit, but there is nothing more that I can do for her now in a direct, physical way, except to make something of what is left of my life - something good, something worthwhile - if I can, as I know how much she would want me to do that, and also to ensure that her name and memory live on, as my personal tribute to a truly wonderful mother and the best person I shall ever know.

Mom is at peace; may my visit to her final resting place on Earth bring me, if still too early for peace yet, at least some degree of acceptance, of understanding regarding our mortality in this present world, in this present life, and also some reaffirment of hope that there is a new life and an everlasting reunion with those we love beyond it, beyond those chained gates that stand before us all during our time here.

1 April 2013, which was also Easter Monday, was the blackest day of my life, because it was the day that my dear mother, Mary Doreen Shuker, passed away.

1 April 2014, exactly one year later, was for me a day of reflection, looking back over what had been a traumatic, life-shattering year of grief, loss, and irrevocable change, but also looking ahead, to whatever the future may hold for me, and to whatever I may accomplish in honour of my mother, and in fulfilment of her most cherished hopes, dreams, and ambitions for me. These contemplations formed the basis of the following composition, written at the closing of that same day..

God bless you, little Mom – thank you for all the happiness, goodness, and love that you have always brought into my life.

A Year Ago Today

Can it be just a year ago today since you passed from my life, my little Mom?

Sometimes it seems but a heartbeat away, other times a thousand lives, a thousand worlds, from where I am now.

People try to show sympathy and understanding when they learn that you have gone, but they have no concept of the true nature of my loss - the immeasurable breadth and limitless depth of the black chasm created in my life and within my heart by your passing. Yes, I have indeed lost my mother - a loss that in itself would be all but unbearable. But I have also lost my best friend, my ever-present housemate, my constant travelling companion, my most trusted confidante, my number one supporter, and my entire family. You were all of those persons, Mom, and so much more besides. Is it any wonder why I grieve without ending, why my life is now but a paltry, meaningless existence, a mere shadow of its former state, why I look only to the past for happiness and security now, and to the future with only loneliness and fear?

I never cried as a child, because I'd never give the school bully, the playground tormentor, the satisfaction of seeing my tears. Instead, I'd save them all, each one a precious pearl of emotion, only to be released in my darkest of all hours some day. Well that day and that hour finally came, a year ago today, the hour in which I lost you, Mom. The tears flowed, and have continued to flow ever since - every tear that I've ever saved throughout my life, torrents of tears that even now after a year of unbroken outpouring continue in unabated profusion, threatening to drown my very being in their salty, burning despair, or to carry me away, borne upon a veritable ocean of tears to who knows where.

I know that your fondest and most fervent wish for me would be that I should make something of my life, do something worthwhile with it, and, most of all, enjoy it, not fill it with grief and sadness. I cannot change the past and bring you back - I would if I could, in an instant, you know that, Mom, but I can't. What I can do, though, is change the future, my future at least, if I choose to do so. You were always so proud of me when you were here, and I can still make you so now. Indeed, it is knowing all of this that has given me a reason, the only reason, to continue day by day through this first year, and it will do so again in those that follow. You sacrificed so much for me, and loved me too much for me to let you down, to betray your faith and your trust in me, and so my books and my articles and my blog posts continue, as you would want and would hope for.

As for me: I am still granted some fleeting but all-the-more-precious moments with you in my dreams, when once again we are together, happy and contented in each other's company as we always were. I still see you in thousands of fondly-recalled memories at home and in millions of happy remembrances within my mind, which help to dispel the ever-present loneliness pervading my world indoors, and bring to me your welcome company to counter the cloud of invisibility that seems to separate me from everyone else whenever I venture forth into the world outdoors.

How truly blessed I am, Mom, to have shared my life with you as my mother for 53 wonderful, happy years, to have been loved unconditionally by someone who was so proud of me and who genuinely thought of me as special, wonderful even. Few people are ever so lucky. I shall always remember that, especially when at my lowest ebb.

This first year of being without you, of being alone in this world, knowing that wherever I look, whichever street I walk along, whatever shop I walk into, I shall never see you again, shall never hear your voice speaking to me again, shall never see your face in the crowd looking for mine again, has been the worst time of my life. Nothing else ever will, ever could, be as devastating, but I shall miss you always, all the days of my life. I now stand on the brink of entering my second year alone, and I can only pray that acceptance will at last be mine, that grief will lift and give me a measure of release, of peace, and that I shall be worthy of you, Mom, that I shall go on to achieve all that you have ever hoped and dreamed for me.

God bless you, little Mom. Please always stay beside me where you always used to be when here, please always give me hope and encouragement as you always used to do when here, and, above all else, please always love me as you always did when here. If you will do these, I will do the rest – this I promise you, Mom, with all my heart and with all my love, always.

How often it is said that Time is a great healer. Two years have gone by since Mom's passing, but for me Time's ministrations have been to no avail – the pain of grief, of loss, of separation, of the grim, heart-wrenching knowledge that I shall never see my mother again in this world remains no less raw, searing, or crippling.

I wrote the following lines to mark the second anniversary of that darkest of all days, and I must keep faith in my cherished belief that through God's good grace one fine bright day not too long coming we shall indeed be together again, with all of our family, forever. I love you, little Mom, always.

If Only...

If only my tears could be the footsteps that lead me to where you have gone.
If only my grief could light my way there, a lantern with which I could see.
If only my faith could bear me upwards to Heaven's bright portal afar.
If only my love could find you waiting, and bring you back homeward with me.

Two years ago today, Mom, you left my life, but you also took it with you.
You left my world, but you also took it with you.
Only your love and my memories remain,
But they are the happiest of companions,
And in my sorrow I must draw upon their shared happiness
To gain some of my own.
If only I could find a way of doing so –
There must be a way, somehow, somewhere...
God bless you, little Mom – how I wish that you were here with me still.
I always will.

When I wrote this poem in late 2012, it had not been a good year for Mom and I, as Mom's health had experienced various age-related setbacks during the preceding months. So I wrote it as my way of expressing what had been, what was then, and what I hoped would be in 2013. Tragically, however, my hopes were not granted, but as I acknowledged in my eulogy to Mom at her funeral, I fully understand and accept God's reason for the path that the future did reveal, even though it took Mom along a very different route from mine, one that will never again intersect with mine in this life. So now I am alone here, and offer up to God the following lines once again, hoping that in His wisdom and grace He will answer them and lead me safely through whatever awaits me in whatever remains to me here.

May It Be

What if I should gain the world, but lose all happiness within it?
What if I should gain immortality, yet lose all those whom I love?
What if I should gain eternity, yet lose you forever, my Lord and Father?
The shadows and darkness have pursued me for so long, O God,
And only you can dispel them and illuminate my life once more.
Hear my voice in the night, calling out to you from the depths of my despair,
Let your benevolence ward off the malevolence encompassing me,
Guide me safely into the welcoming light of morning,
And may the salvation and peace that I seek be mine at last.

My mother, aged early/mid-20s (© Mary D. Shuker/Dr Karl Shuker)

My mother and I in the Cat Street galleries, Hong Kong, summer 2005 (© Dr Karl Shuker)

INDEX OF TITLES

ACKNOWLEDGEMENTS

First and foremost, I thank with all my heart my family, for their inspiration, guidance, encouragement, and love – without whom and without which I could have accomplished nothing. I only wish that they could all still be here with me today, as they were when I was writing many of the poems in this book, but I draw great comfort from the words of a Hebrew proverb: "Say not in grief: 'They are no more', but live in thankfulness that they were". I do, and shall continue to do so all the days of my life.

I also wish to thank those kind souls down through the years who have read my poetry and commented favourably but fairly upon it, and whose words stayed within my mind until at last they stirred me into preparing this collection's original edition for publication. In particular, I am very grateful for the encouraging thoughts of fellow Midlands-based poet Glynnis Briscoe after reading a selection of my poetry many moons ago, and one of whose works of prose inspired my poem 'A Last Visit'.

That in turn leads me to thank very sincerely my old friend Jonathan Downes for making that original publication happen, as well as this new edition, and in so doing adding a very different genre to the CFZ Press's ever-expanding catalogue and diversity of books.

Finally, I wish to thank an old school friend of mine, Nigel Parton, for producing the delightful illustration that appears on the front cover of both editions of this book, inspiring their title, and which has an interesting little story all of its own.

Entitled 'Star Steed', it is a scraperboard picture that Nigel prepared when we were both around 16 years old. I liked it so much that I purchased it from him for the then-princely sum of £5, and proudly framed it for my bedroom. I also wrote a corresponding poem,

'The Star Horse', inspired by it (and now also included in this book), which I gave to Nigel as an additional payment, ever since when 'Star Steed' has remained framed and on display here at home. Following the publication of this book's first edition in 2009, I was delighted to receive an email from Nigel, our first contact for over 30 years, and to learn from him that he still remembered preparing 'Star Steed'.

ABOUT THE AUTHOR

Born and still living in the West Midlands, England, Dr Karl P.N. Shuker graduated from the University of Leeds with a Bachelor of Science (Honours) degree in pure zoology, and from the University of Birmingham with a Doctor of Philosophy degree in zoology and comparative physiology. He now works full-time as a freelance zoological consultant to the media, and as a prolific published writer.

Dr Shuker is currently the author of 23 books and hundreds of articles, principally on animal-related subjects, with an especial interest in cryptozoology and animal mythology, on which he is an internationally-recognised authority, but also including the present volume of poetry's two editions. In addition, he has acted as consultant for several major multi-contributor volumes as well as for the world-renowned *Guinness Book of Records/Guinness World Records* (he is currently its Senior Consultant for its Life Sciences section), and he has compiled questions for the BBC's long-running cerebral quiz 'Mastermind'. He is also the editor of the *Journal of Cryptozoology*, the world's only peer-reviewed scientific journal dedicated to mystery animals.

Dr Shuker has travelled the world in the course of his researches and writings, and has appeared regularly on television and radio. Aside from work, his diverse range of interests include motorbikes, the life and career of James Dean, collecting masquerade and carnival masks, quizzes, philately, poetry, travel, world mythology, and the history of animation.

He is a Scientific Fellow of the prestigious Zoological Society of London, a Fellow of the Royal Entomological Society, a Member of the International Society of Cryptozoology and other wildlife-related organisations, he is Cryptozoology Consultant to the Centre for Fortean Zoology, and is also a Member of the Society of Authors.

Dr Shuker's personal website can be accessed at http://www.karlshuker.com and he has an extremely popular anomalous wildlife/animal mythology blog, ShukerNature (at: http://www.karlshuker.blogspot.com), a separate blog, Star Steeds, devoted to his poetry (at: http://www.starsteeds.blogspot.com), and a third blog, The Eclectarium of Doctor Shuker, devoted to his diverse interests outside wildlife and poetry (at: http://www.eclectariumshuker.blogspot.com). There is also an entry for Dr Shuker in the online encyclopedia Wikipedia, and a fan page on Facebook.

The author with *Smilodon* skull (© Dr Karl Shuker)

AUTHOR BIBLIOGRAPHY

Mystery Cats of the World: From Blue Tigers To Exmoor Beasts (Robert Hale: London, 1989)

Extraordinary Animals Worldwide (Robert Hale: London, 1991)

The Lost Ark: New and Rediscovered Animals of the 20th Century (HarperCollins: London, 1993)

Dragons: A Natural History (Aurum: London/Simon & Schuster: New York, 1995; republished Taschen: Cologne, 2006)

In Search of Prehistoric Survivors: Do Giant 'Extinct' Creatures Still Exist? (Blandford: London, 1995)

The Unexplained: An Illustrated Guide to the World's Natural and Paranormal Mysteries (Carlton: London/JG Press: North Dighton, 1996; republished Carlton: London, 2002)

From Flying Toads To Snakes With Wings: From the Pages of FATE Magazine (Llewellyn: St Paul, 1997; republished Bounty: London, 2005)

Mysteries of Planet Earth: An Encyclopedia of the Inexplicable (Carlton: London, 1999)

The Hidden Powers of Animals: Uncovering the Secrets of Nature (Reader's Digest: Pleasantville/Marshall Editions: London, 2001)

The New Zoo: New and Rediscovered Animals of the Twentieth Century [fully-updated, greatly-expanded, new edition of *The Lost Ark*] (House of Stratus Ltd: Thirsk, UK/House of Stratus Inc: Poughkeepsie, USA, 2002)

The Beasts That Hide From Man: Seeking the World's Last Undiscovered Animals (Paraview: New York, 2003)

Extraordinary Animals Revisited: From Singing Dogs To Serpent Kings (CFZ Press: Bideford, 2007)

Dr Shuker's Casebook: In Pursuit of Marvels and Mysteries (CFZ Press: Bideford, 2008)

Dinosaurs and Other Prehistoric Animals on Stamps: A Worldwide Catalogue (CFZ Press: Bideford, 2008)

Star Steeds and Other Dreams: The Collected Poems (CFZ Press: Bideford, 2009)

Karl Shuker's Alien Zoo: From the Pages of Fortean Times (CFZ Press: Bideford, 2010).

The Encyclopaedia of New and Rediscovered Animals: From The Lost Ark to The New Zoo – and Beyond [fully-updated, greatly-expanded, third edition of *The Lost Ark*] (Coachwhip Publications: Landisville, 2012).

Cats of Magic, Mythology, and Mystery: A Feline Phantasmagoria (CFZ Press: Bideford, 2012).

Mirabilis: A Carnival of Cryptozoology and Unnatural History (Anomalist Books: San Antonio, 2013).

Dragons in Zoology, Cryptozoology, and Culture (Coachwhip Publications: Greenville, 2013).

The Menagerie of Marvels: A Third Compendium of Extraordinary Animals (CFZ Press: Bideford, 2014).

A Manifestation of Monsters: Examining the (Un)Usual Suspects (Anomalist Books: San Antonio, 2015).

More Star Steeds and Other Dreams: The Collected Poems – New, Expanded Edition (CFZ Press: Bideford, 2015).

Consultant and also Contributor
Man and Beast (Reader's Digest: Pleasantville, New York, 1993)

Secrets of the Natural World (Reader's Digest: Pleasantville, New York, 1993)

Almanac of the Uncanny (Reader's Digest: Surry Hills, Australia, 1995)

The Guinness Book of Records/Guinness World Records 1998-present day (Guinness: London, 1997-present day)

Consultant
Monsters (Lorenz: London, 2001)

Contributor
Of Monsters and Miracles CD-ROM (Croydon Museum/Interactive Designs: Oxton, 1995)

Fortean Times Weird Year 1996 (John Brown Publishing: London, 1996)

Mysteries of the Deep (Llewellyn: St Paul, 1998)

Guinness Amazing Future (Guinness: London, 1999)

The Earth (Channel 4 Books: London, 2000)

Mysteries and Monsters of the Sea (Gramercy: New York, 2001)

Chambers Dictionary of the Unexplained (Chambers: Edinburgh, 2007)

Chambers Myths and Mysteries (Chambers: Edinburgh, 2008)

The Fortean Times Paranormal Handbook (Dennis Publishing: London, 2009).

Plus numerous contributions to the annual *CFZ Yearbook* series of volumes.

Editor
Journal of Cryptozoology (the world's only peer-reviewed scientific journal dedicated to mystery animals, published by CFZ Press).

HOW TO START A PUBLISHING EMPIRE

Unlike most mainstream publishers, we have a non-commercial remit, and our mission statement claims that "we publish books because they deserve to be published, not because we think that we can make money out of them". Our motto is the Latin Tag *Pro bona causa facimus* (we do it for good reason), a slogan taken from a children's book *The Case of the Silver Egg* by the late Desmond Skirrow.

WIKIPEDIA: "The first book published was in 1988. *Take this Brother may it Serve you Well* was a guide to Beatles bootlegs by Jonathan Downes. It sold quite well, but was hampered by very poor production values, being photocopied, and held together by a plastic clip binder.

In 1988 A5 clip binders were hard to get hold of, so the publishers took A4 binders and cut them in half with a hacksaw. It now reaches surprisingly high prices second hand.

The production quality improved slightly over the years, and after 1999 all the books produced were ringbound with laminated colour covers. In 2004, however, they signed an agreement with Lightning Source, and all books are now produced perfect bound, with full colour covers."

Until 2010 all our books, the majority of which are/were on the subject of mystery animals and allied disciplines, were published by `CFZ Press`, the publishing arm of the Centre for Fortean Zoology (CFZ), and we urged our readers and followers to draw a discreet veil over the books that we published that were completely off topic to the CFZ.

However, in 2010 we decided that enough was enough and launched a second imprint, `Fortean Words` which aims to cover a wide range of non animal-related esoteric subjects. Other imprints will be launched as and when we feel like it, however the basic ethos of the company remains the same: Our job is to publish books and magazines that we feel are worth publishing, whether or not they are going to sell. Money is, after all - as my dear old Mama once told me - a rather vulgar subject, and she would be rolling in her grave if she thought that her eldest son was somehow in `trade`.

Luckily, so far our tastes have turned out not to be that rarified after all, and we have sold far more books than anyone ever thought that we would, so there is a moral in there somewhere...

Jon Downes,
Woolsery, North Devon
July 2010

CFZ PRESS

CFZ Press is our flagship imprint, featuring a wide range of intelligently written and lavishly illustrated books on cryptozoology and the quirkier aspects of Natural History.

CFZ Classics is a new venture for us. There are many seminal works that are either unavailable today, or not available with the production values which we would like to see. So, following the old adage that if you want to get something done do it yourself, this is exactly what we have done.

Desiderius Erasmus Roterodamus (b. October 18th 1466, d. July 2nd 1536) said: "When I have a little money, I buy books; and if I have any left, I buy food and clothes," and we are much the same. Only, we are in the lucky position of being able to share our books with the wider world. CFZ Classics is a conduit through which we cannot just re-issue titles which we feel still have much to offer the cryptozoological and Fortean research communities of the 21st Century, but we are adding footnotes, supplementary essays, and other material where we deem it appropriate.

http://www.cfzpublishing.co.uk/

Fortean Words is a new venture for us. The F in CFZ stands for "Fortean", after the pioneering researcher into anomalous phenomena, Charles Fort. Our Fortean Words imprint covers a whole spectrum of arcane subjects from UFOs and the paranormal to folklore and urban legends. Our authors include such Fortean luminaries as Nick Redfern, Andy Roberts, and Paul Screeton. . New authors tackling new subjects will always be encouraged, and we hope that our books will continue to be as ground-breaking and popular as ever.

Just before Christmas 2011, we launched our third imprint, this time dedicated to - let's see if you guessed it from the title - fictional books with a Fortean or cryptozoological theme. We have published a few fictional books in the past, but now think that because of our rising reputation as publishers of quality Forteana, that a dedicated fiction imprint was the order of the day.

http://www.cfzpublishing.co.uk/

www.ingramcontent.com/pod-product-compliance
Lightning Source LLC
Chambersburg PA
CBHW051818090426
42736CB00011B/1536